CHRISTMAS AROUND THE WORLD

Table of Contents

Teacher Input Suggestions .... 2 - 4

List of Resources .... 4 - 5

Introductory Lesson .... 6 - 7

Jordan .... 8 - 11

Finland .... 12 - 15

The Netherlands .... 16 - 18

Germany .... 19 - 25

Brazil .... 26 - 29

Sweden .... 30 - 34

Poland .... 35 - 39

Austria .... 40 - 43

Japan .... 44 - 46

Italy .... 47 - 50

Norway .... 51 - 54

Denmark .... 55 - 59

Greece .... 60 - 65

Mexico and Spain .... 66 - 70

France .... 71 - 73

Commonwealth of Independent States (C.I.S) .... 74 - 79

Canada, the United States and Great Britain .... 80 - 91

CHRISTMAS AROUND THE WORLD

Teacher Input Suggestions

1. Display a map of the world and label names of countries to be studied. Perhaps countries could be printed on small bell shapes or wreaths, or Christmas trees, etc.

2. Have a nature study of Christmas trees. Take a walk around the neighbourhood to observe the different kinds of Christmas trees native to the area or popularly used for holiday purposes in the area. Point out the differences in the various evergreens to the students. If possible, collect pine cones for use in classroom art projects.

3. Have the students plan a Christmas party. Set up groups to work on refreshments (perhaps have cooking sessions to prepare tasty things), decorations, and entertainment.

4. Have each student trace the shape of their hand on red or green construction paper. Spell the word "PEACE" using these "hands" on a bulletin board display with the heading "OUR WISH FOR THE WORLD".

5. Make a bulletin board display entitled "SEASONS GREETINGS FROM OTHER LANDS". Write "Merry Christmas" in several different languages. (See lesson on Poland)

6. Set up a Christmas learning centre with books related to the theme. For example place story books, song books, cook books, and poetry at the centre. Books can help your students enjoy and experience the joy and true meaning of the season.

7. Make a Christmas puzzle mural. Divide a piece of white mural paper into as many pieces as you have students. Cut out the pieces and distribute one to each student. They are to colour a 2 cm border using a black marker. The students then illustrate a picture depicting

CHRISTMAS AROUND THE WORLD

Christmas customs in various countries throughout the world.

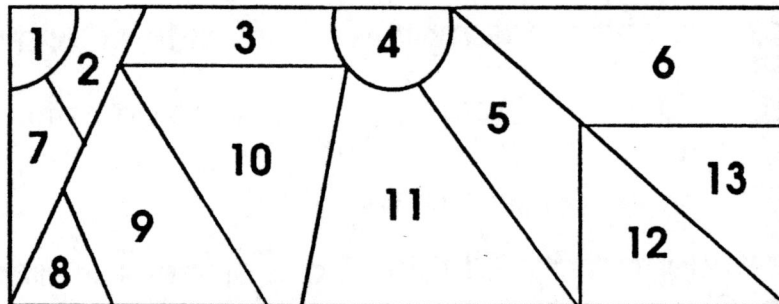

8. Make a picture collage of "Christmas Around the World" using magazines and newspaper clippings.

9. Have students prepare an oral presentation on Christmas in a specific country. Have them dress accordingly and either videotape the results or capture their presentation on slides.

10. Working in small groups have the students prepare puppet plays depicting Christmas customs and traditions in other lands. Make and decorate appropriate hand puppets. Design a backdrop.

11. Make available records and/or cassettes of Christmas music of all kinds.

12. Foster an understanding of other customs by organizing and performing a Christmas play for the school to enjoy. One very appropriate one is entitled "Christmas Around the World" by Betsy Coffin and Beverly Lindholm. This can be found in Instructor Magazine November/December 1982.

13. Read and tell Christmas stories and poems, both traditional and modern. Some suggestions are the following:

   a) A Visit from St. Nicholas by Clement Moore

   b) Mousekin's Christmas Eve by Edna Miller

   c) A Green Christmas by Theodora Kroeber

CHRISTMAS AROUND THE WORLD

 d) <u>Baboushka and the Three Kings</u> by Ruth Robbins

 e) Any one of the many versions of the Christmas story.

14. Read <u>The Elves and the Shoemaker</u> and supplement it with <u>The Elves"
   Christmas Eve</u> found in The Magic of Music, Book One, Ginn. A musical
   dramatization could be prepared.

15. Have your students make Christmas decorations of all kinds that are
   symbolic of Christmas in various countries.

   For example:

   glittering stars (Finland)   paper ornament chains (Poland)
   tinsel tail birds (Brazil)
   pinata (Mexico and Spain)
   stained glass windows (Italy)

   List of Resources

Barth, Edna. <u>Reindeer and Colored Lights</u>. Houghton ; ©1971

Barth, Edna. <u>A Christmas Feast: Poems, Sayings, Greetings and Wishes</u>.
Houghton; © 1979

Fowler, Virginie. <u>Christmas Crafts and Customs Around the World</u>. Simon
and Schuster; ©1984

Harper, Kenn. <u>Christmas in the Big Igloo.</u> Outcrop Ltd.; ©1983

Hazeltine, Alice I. and Smith, Elva S. <u>The Christmas Book of Legends and
Stories</u>. Lothrop, Lee and Shepard Co.; ©1944

Herda, D.J. <u>Christmas</u>. Watts; ©1983

CHRISTMAS AROUND THE WORLD

Johnson, Lois. Christmas Stories Round the World. Rand McNally & Co.; ©1960

Sechrist, Elizabeth Hough. Christmas Everywhere. MacRae Smith Co.; ©1962

Stevens, Patricia B. Merry Christmas: A History of the Holiday. Macmillan; ©1979

Wilson, Robina B. Merry Christmas: Children at Christmas Around the World. Putnam; ©1983

CHRISTMAS AROUND THE WORLD

Christmas is that special time of year for people to be with families and friends. Many families have special ways of celebrating Christmas whether it be by exchanging presents, decorating homes, singing carols, serving special foods, or attending special church services. People in different countries have their own favourite Christmas traditions. Christmas is a time to remember that people all over the world are alike in many ways even though different countries all have different customs.

Find out all the wonderful things that can happen in the countries listed below. Print them on the map of the world.

Jordan	Norway	Finland	Denmark	Greece
Mexico	Germany	Spain	Brazil	The Netherlands
Sweden	France	Poland	Great Britain	United States
Canada	Japan	Austria	Italy	

Commonwealth of Independent States

Remember although customs and traditions may differ from country to country, boys and girls are much alike everywhere.

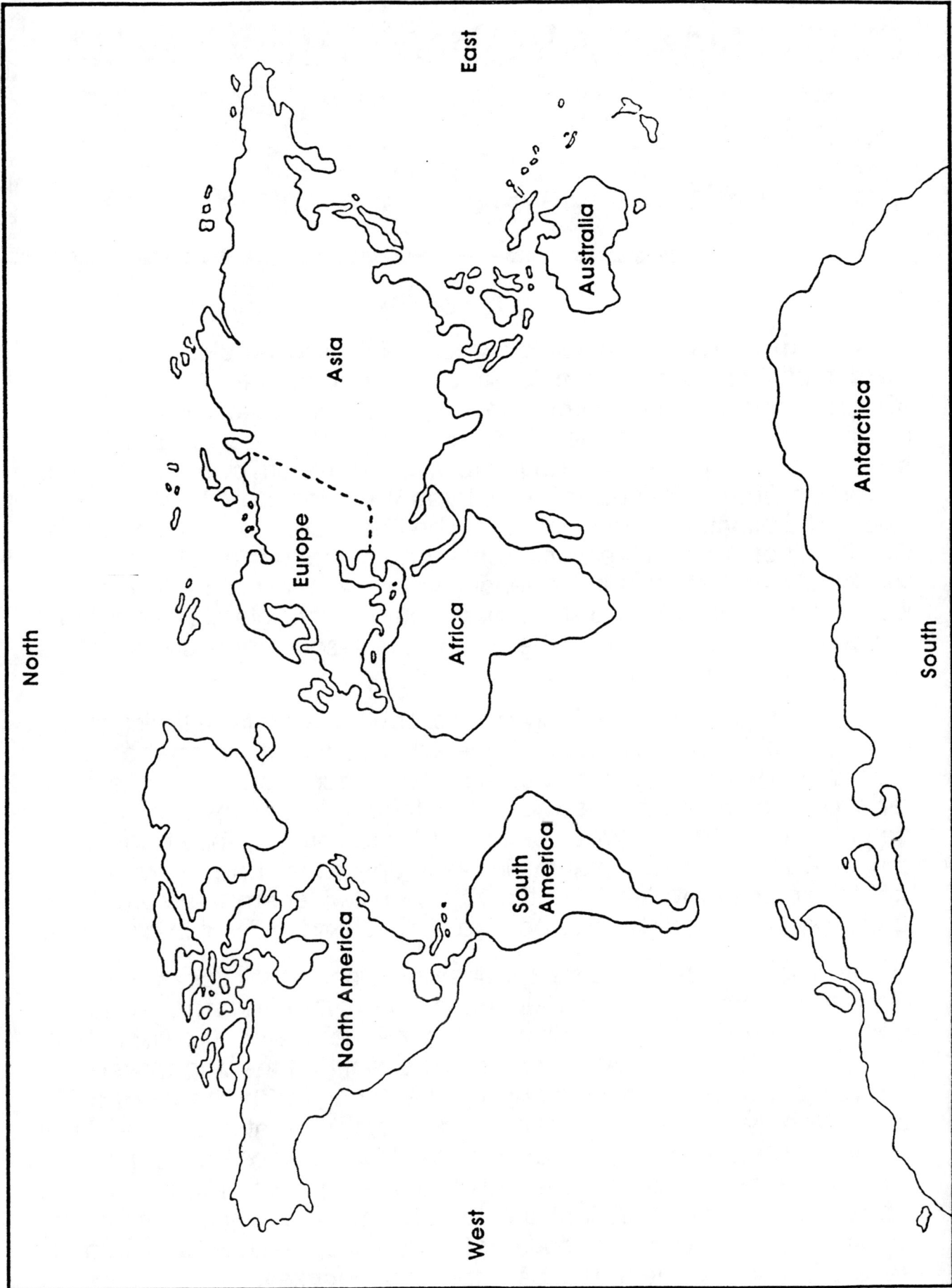

North

East

West

South

Asia

Europe

Africa

Australia

Antarctica

North America

South America

CHRISTMAS AROUND THE WORLD

Jordan

Christmas is a religious holiday which celebrates the birth of Jesus Christ. Most Christians observe Christmas on December the 25th. The story of Christmas comes mainly from the Gospels of Saint Luke and Saint Matthew in the New Testament. Luke tells the story of how an angel appeared to shepherds outside the town of Bethlehem and told them of the birth of Jesus. Matthew tells how Three Wise Men, called Magi, followed a bright star that led them to the Baby Jesus. On Christmas Eve, Christians from all over the world come together for a special religious service at midnight mass in Bethlehem which is known as the Holy Land. It is a town in Jordan about 8 km (5 miles) south of Jerusalem. People kneel to kiss a silver star that is set in the ground at the spot where Jesus' birth is believed to have taken place.

According to the story, Mary and Joseph travelled from their Nazareth home to Bethlehem on December the 24th because the master of the then known world, Augustus Caesar, issued a decree ordering a general registration of all his subjects. This was for the purpose of revising or completing the tax lists. When Mary and Joseph arrived, they had no shelter. There was no room at the inn, or khan. So they had to stay in a stable, a place provided for cattle. And so in Bethlehem, Jesus was born and Mary "wrapped Him in swaddling clothes, and laid Him in a manger".

Tradition tells us that as the shepherds watched their flocks on this night, they were dazzled by a light more brilliant than the stars. Angels appeared singing the glad tidings. These shepherds were the first to hear and spread the news. It is because of this event that the angels were heralding, that people rejoice and join the throng of Christians in the City of the Nativity each year. It is also because of this event that there is today so much "peace on earth" and "good will toward men". During the Christmas season, many homes and churches display a crèche or Nativity scene showing figures of Mary and Joseph watching over the Infant Jesus in the stable, surrounded by figures of angels, shepherds, Wise Men and several animals - some sheep, perhaps, and a donkey.

CHRISTMAS AROUND THE WORLD

Gift giving is an important part of Christmas because when Jesus was born, the shepherds and Three Wise Men wanted to show their love by bringing Him gifts. The shepherds brought such things as fruit, honey, and a white dove. The Three Wise Men brought precious gifts of gold, frankincense, and myrrh.

CHRISTMAS AROUND THE WORLD

Jordan

I ABC Order:

Put the following words in alphabetical order then write their meanings. Use a dictionary to help you.

shepherd	decree	khan	swaddling
manger	tradition	tidings	heralding
throng	frankincense	myrrh	

II Once Upon a Christmas Time:

Retell the story of the first Christmas experience from the point of view of **one** of the following:

    a) a poor shepherd boy
    b) Mary or Joseph
    c) One of the Wise Men

III Poetry:

Write an acrostic poem telling the story of Christmas using the letters of Jordan to start each line of your poem:

e.g.   J - _____

        O - _____

        R - _____

        D - _____

        A - _____

        N - _____

CHRISTMAS AROUND THE WORLD

IV Diorama:

Using a shoebox, create a diorama depicting the Nativity scene.

Make figures from clay, paper maché, or plasticine. Include figures of the Baby Jesus, Mary, Joseph, several animals, shepherds, Wise Men, and angels.

CHRISTMAS AROUND THE WORLD

Finland

The Finnish people begin the Christmas season on the last Sunday in November which is known as "Little Christmas". At this time the marketplaces begin to display majestic trees while families start their celebrations at home with a big party. Songs are sung and everyone eats Christmas pudding and gingerbread snaps. Some of the traditional tree ornaments are made on "Little Christmas" day.

One custom that is practised by some Finnish people is suspending straw from the ceiling and decorating it lovingly with hanging paper stars. Some people use a net-like piece of fabric instead of the straw. The stars reflect the light from candles and lamps which make the suspended ceiling look like a starlit sky. This custom is known as "Finnish Heaven".

On Christmas Eve, December 24th, they put up and decorate the Christmas tree with candy wrapped in foil, apples, cookies, paper stars, tinsel and candles. The family then visits a sauna to cleanse themselves. This is a century old tradition and the Finnish are known to be meticulously clean. After their cleansing ritual everyone dresses in their best clothes and then they return home for the festivities which include a feast of porridge, cold ham, roast pig, mashed and boiled potatoes, pickled herring, red cabbage, rice, fish, turnip pudding and other favourite fishes.

Following this scrumptious meal, comes the big event for the children. Father Christmas or Santa Claus arrives from Lapland with presents. Then everyone usually goes to bed as they must arise early for church services.

Christmas Day is basically very quiet and family orientated. The menu for Christmas dinner is usually roast pig and rice pudding which has one almond as a gesture of good luck for the new year to come.

On December the 26th, St. Stephen's Day, the Finnish people enjoy horseracing and visiting friends and relatives. The culmination to this festive day is a dance.

CHRISTMAS AROUND THE WORLD

Finland

I Stars In Your Eyes

The Finnish star is sure to adorn every home in Finland. **What is a star?** The dictionary describes it as a self-luminous heavenly body visible from earth on a clear night.

Stars dazzle and twinkle on many a Christmas tree throughout the world. Many people put a large illuminated star on the very top of their tree. It is a reminder of the Star of Bethlehem.

A There are numerous "star" words one might find in the dictionary. Read the lists which follows, then write a meaning for each.

starlight	stardom	starry-eyed
starling	stargaze	starfish
starboard	starry	star-spangled
startle	starveling	starlet

star of Bethlehem (two meanings)

B Now put your "star"ry words in ABC order.

C Write the words from the list that are compound words.

D Tell what you think each of these "star" iffic sayings mean:

1. reach for the stars
2. stars in your eyes
3. a star is born

CHRISTMAS AROUND THE WORLD

Finland

II Three Wishes

"I wish I may, I wish I might, I wish upon a star tonight..."

Christmas is a time for wishing. If you could make three wishes at Christmas time, what would they be?

Write your wishes in the stars provided. On the large star write your story about how your life changed when one of these wishes actually came true.

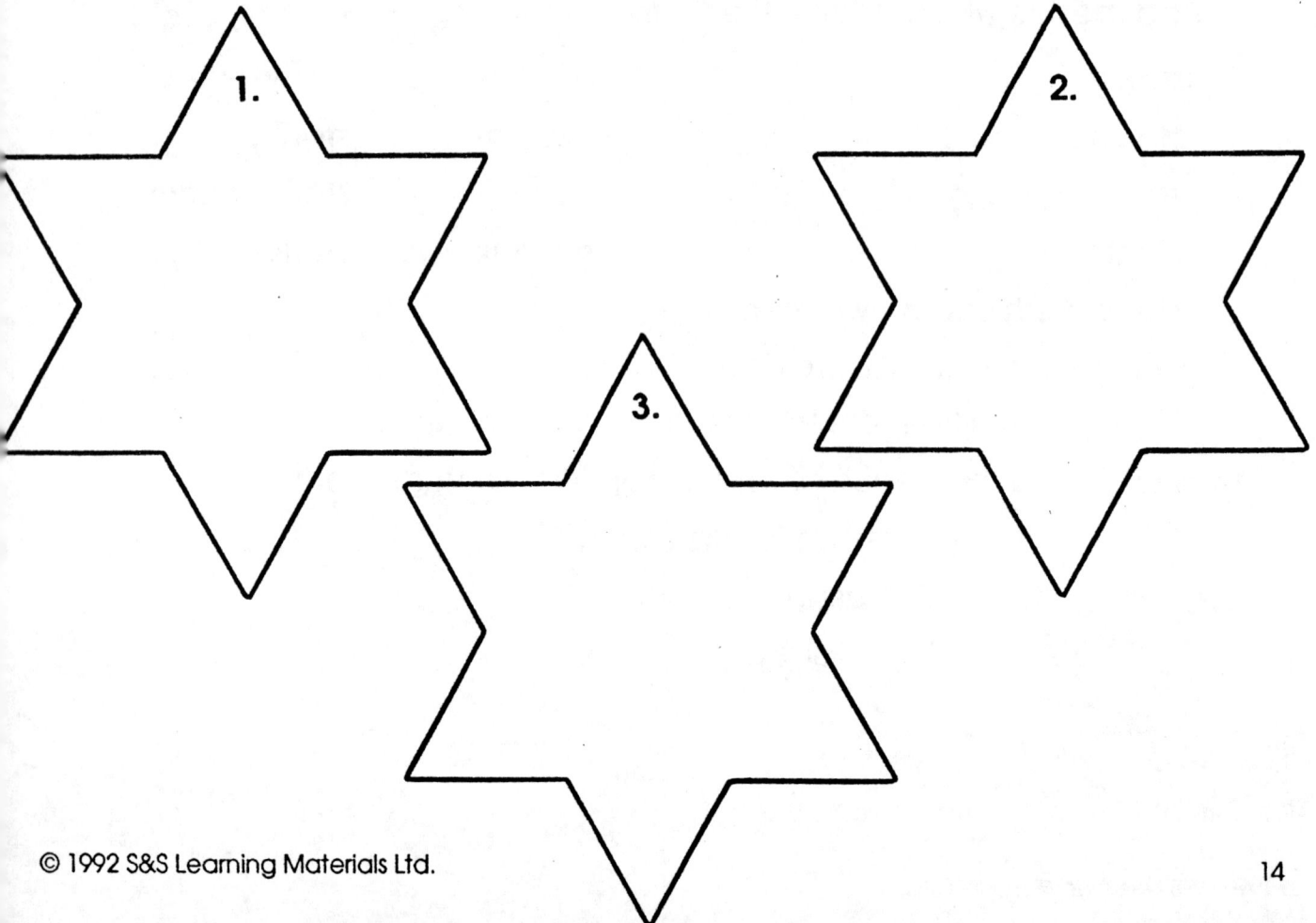

1.

2.

3.

Finland

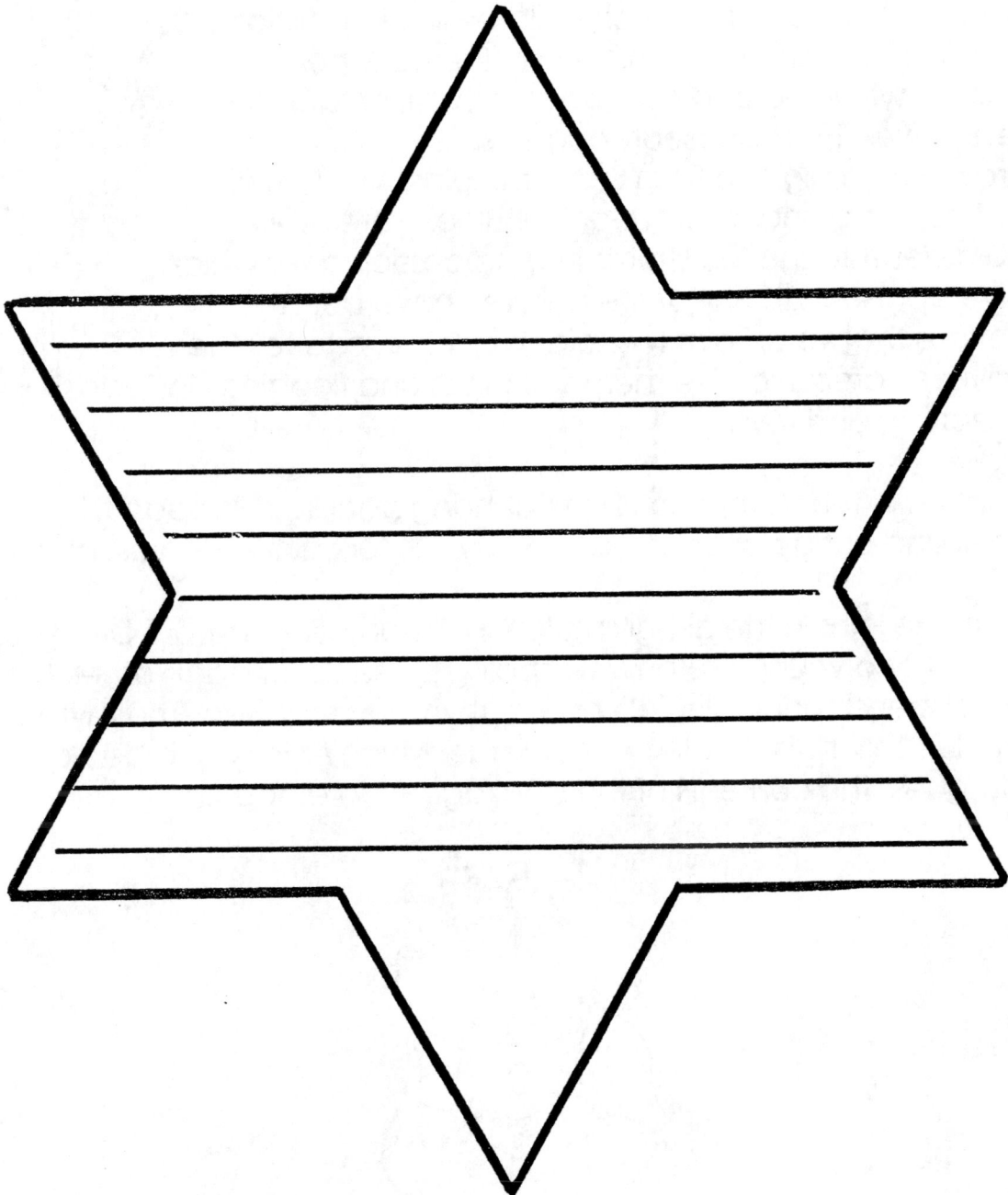

CHRISTMAS AROUND THE WORLD

The Netherlands

The birth of Saint Nicholas is celebrated in the Netherlands (Holland) on December the 6th. The Dutch children like to call Saint Nicholas "Sinter Klass". He wears embroidered robes, embellished with gold and gems, has a mitre, crosier and jewelled gloves. He supposedly comes sailing into Amsterdam on a big ship from Spain bringing with him his great white horse and his companion, Black Peter. Saint Nicholas rides through the streets in a procession after which he delivers presents. If any of the children have been mischievous that year, Saint Nicholas is quite sure to tell them and advises parents to give them scoldings and floggings instead of confections and toys.

Children in the Netherlands do not hang stockings. Instead they set out shoes and put a carrot and some hay out for Saint Nicholas' horse.

Everyone joins in the gift-giving fun. For many days before December the 6th, old and young are busy wrapping presents for each other. On each wrapper a special jingle, verse or rhyme is attached. The rhyme gives a clue to what is inside the package. Much revelry is to be had trying to guess the contents of the package before opening it.

CHRISTMAS AROUND THE WORLD

The Netherlands

I Match the words in Column **A** with their meanings in Column **B**.

Column A	Column B
1. mitre	____ impish
2. crosier	____ candies
3. embroider	____ made beautiful
4. floggings	____ beatings
5. confections	____ group of people walking
6. scolding	____ to decorate with needlework
7. procession	____ merry-making
8. revelry	____ tall cap
9. embellished	____ staff
10. mischievous	____ finding fault with

II All Wrapped Up:

A tradition that the Dutch follow each Christmas is to write a rhyme on the outside of each wrapped present. The rhyme gives a hint as to what is inside the package.

For example: **I'm wooden with a string,**
                   My shape is round
                   Up and down I go,
                   But I make no sound
                              (a yo yo)

CHRISTMAS AROUND THE WORLD

Pretend that you have your Christmas shopping all wrapped up. Think of what you would give to three special people in your life. On the three boxes provided write a rhyme or jingle hinting at the contents of each of the packages.

CHRISTMAS AROUND THE WORLD

Germany

The Germans prepare for Christmas well in advance. Saint Nicholas Eve on December the 6th is the beginning of the Christmas season which continues until the Twelfth Night on January the 6th. Stores and markets are festively decorated and displayed with beautiful Christmas decorations. The Germans were one of the first peoples to make the gorgeous decorations and tree ornaments that are now a part of Christmas customs throughout the world.

One common decoration in Germany is known as the "Little Prune Man". His body is a big fig and his arms, legs and feet are made from raisins and prunes. His head is a walnut. Another favourite is called the "Crackling Gold Angel". As the legend goes the angel is a reminder of a particular dollmaker who made an angel for his wife. The angel looked exactly like their daughter who had died.

Besides decorations, many of the world's Christmas traditions originated in Germany - the most renowned being the Christmas tree or Tannenbaum. The German mother usually decorates the Christmas tree, in secret, on Christmas Eve, December the 24th. She uses beautiful glass balls, tinsel and cookies such as Kringelor which are transparent sugar cookies made in the shape of figure eights. The tree was also adorned with spicy cakes made in various shapes. These are called Lebkuchen. Other favourite tree "treats" are Stöllen and Pfefferkuchen. Liibecker marzipan fruits and vegetables are also popular. When the tree was completed the rest of the family would see it for the first time.

In the early days, Saint Nicholas, the giver of gifts would arrive on a white horse on December the 6th to distribute presents to the children who were good. With him came a small servant named Krampus who would bring switches or rods for the children who didn't behave. Later on, the children began to write their letters to the Christkind, who was believed to be a messenger of Jesus. He is dressed in a white robe and wears a golden crown and has golden wings.

CHRISTMAS AROUND THE WORLD

The children would decorate their letter with sugar which they adhered by using glue. Traditionally, candles are lit in their windows to help the Christkind find his way.

The Christkind arrives on Christmas Eve. With him is a companion, adorned in fur, known to the German people as Prince Ruprecht or Ruklas. His job is twofold. First he spies on the children prior to Christmas to see who is good. Secondly he helps the Christkind by taking the gifts down the chimney. On Christmas Day, the children are excited to see what the Christkind has brought them.

CHRISTMAS AROUND THE WORLD

Germany

Festive Treats

Besides the Christmas tree, numerous other Christmas traditions came from Germany. The Advent Wreath, the Christmas crib, many traditional foods, symbols and music all originated in Germany. The very first picture of Santa Claus in the United States was illustrated by a German artist. Germany is indeed a nation rich in Christmas lore.

One tradition that we all relish are Christmas cookies which are ever so popular the world over. As you have read the Germans make cookies such as Lebkuchen, Stöllen, Pfefferkuchen and Marzipan. Cookies are cut out in many forms and shapes - animals, fruits and vegetables to name a few.

Below you will find a recipe for Marzipan cookies. Read the ingredients and the method. Then underline six action words or verbs that you find in the method and then put them in the cookie shapes provided.

For example: Eat your cookie before it crumbles.

(eat and crumbles are action words)

Marzipan Cookies

Ingredients:

    1   cup of butter or margarine
    1/2 cup of sugar
    21/2 cups of all purpose flour
    1/2 tsp. of almond extract
         food colouring

CHRISTMAS AROUND THE WORLD

Method:

Cream the butter and sugar. Stir in the flour and almond extract. Divide the mixture into three equal parts. Colour and make the mixture into shapes. Place cookies on an ungreased baking sheet. Chill for about thirty minutes. Bake in an 300ºF (150º C) for 1/2 hour.

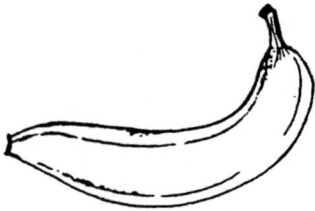

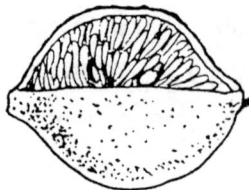

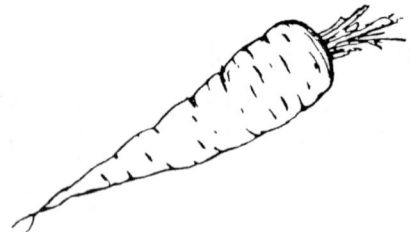

Perhaps you could try to make these cookies at home. I'm sure the results would be a sweet success.

B Search through some recipe books and in your best writing copy a recipe for another type of German cookie and underline the action words.

CHRISTMAS AROUND THE WORLD

Germany

II Oh Christmas Tree

One of the most charming and beautiful symbols of Christmas is, of course, the Christmas tree. Though some are simply adorned and others are sophisticated and glamorous, they all capture the essence and the splendour of a treasured time of the year. We gaze with admiration at the vision of beauty it portrays.

There are numerous legends as to the origin of this majestic tree. One legend tells of a poor forester and his family who helped a child who happened to be the Christ Child. This child touched a fir tree beside their humble home and this special tree became the very first Christmas tree.

Another legend tells of three trees that were near the stable where Jesus was born. One was a date palm, one was an olive tree and yet another was a pine tree. The date palm gave dates as a gift to the Baby Jesus, the olive tree gave olives. However, the pine tree had no gift at all. The stars in the sky above took pity on the pine tree and they descended onto its branches, glowing majestically for the Baby Jesus and, as the legend goes, this marked the beginning of the traditional Christmas tree.

Still another story circles around a German missionary called Winfred who was later known as St. Boniface. It is said that when Winfred cut down an oak tree, a fir tree immediately came up in its place. He was startled by this miracle and he surmised that the tree was a symbol from the Christ Child.

Another story tells about a man named Martin Luther who lived in Germany. One Christmas Eve, he was walking through a snow covered woods on a clear starry night when he suddenly had what he thought was a fabulous idea. He decided to cut down a fir tree, carry it home and decorate it with candles. His children were ecstatic with the results.

CHRISTMAS AROUND THE WORLD

Despite these many legends about the origin of the Christmas tree, it probably developed years ago in Germany from the "Paradise tree" -which is a type of evergreen. As far back as 1605 Germans used evergreens to decorate their homes. Wherever the German people moved, they brought with them the tradition. In fact the first Christmas trees in North America were used by German settlers in the 1800's. What ever its origin, the heritage of the Christmas tree is one that will be passed on to generations to come.

Shed some light on the origin of the Christmas tree by writing your very own legend about the first Christmas tree. Tap your imagination and come up with a "tree"-mendously convincing story.

Write your legend on the tree shape provided.

CHRISTMAS AROUND THE WORLD

CHRISTMAS AROUND THE WORLD

Brazil

In Brazil, Christmas comes in mid-summer rather than in mid-winter. Consequently, Brazilians celebrate with festivals, picnics, boating and, of course, going to the beach. Christmas festivities run from December the 24th to January the 6th.

The Brazilian people decorate and display their homemade "presebres". A "presebre" is basically the traditional manger scene which reminds the people of Jesus' birth. Many of the homecrafted figurines in the presebre are handed down from past generations but some figurines are newly crafted by the children and these too will remain in the family to be passed along to future generations.

Brazilians decorate their homes with beautiful red flowers and green eucalyptus leaves. Green and red commonly used by many countries have much significance. The green represents the passage of winter and the red symbolizes the blood of Christ.

On December the 24th, Christmas Eve, there are many open air dances and festivals. Before going to Mass the families prepare and set the table with a huge meal which they will eat upon returning from Mass. Some foods one might eat if celebrating with a Brazilian family are: fried shrimp, fish pie, roast pig, turkey and numerous desserts. When they leave for church they take with them a "white-gift" which is an item of food for the poor wrapped in white paper.

Upon returning from church, the family feasts on their festive meal and then gathers to see their tree for the first time. The tree is then lit up with the many candles that adorn it. The family sings Christmas carols. Afterwards it is time for the children to prepare for Papa Noël (Sao Nicolau). He always leaves gifts in the shoes that they gleefully put out for him. He also hides gifts throughout the house.

CHRISTMAS AROUND THE WORLD

When the children arise on Christmas morning, it is the tradition to serve their parents breakfast in bed before discovering what Papa Noël brought for them.

CHRISTMAS AROUND THE WORLD

Brazil

I A Christmas An "noun" cement!

A noun is the name of a person, place or a thing.

For example: <u>Jane</u> went to <u>Brazil</u> for <u>Christmas</u>.

Nouns - Jane (person)

Brazil (place)

Christmas (thing - holiday)

From the information given on Christmas in Brazil find **ten** nouns and write them in the spaces provided. In parentheses tell whether the noun represents a person, a place or a thing.

1. _____ (_____)

2. _____ (_____)

3. _____ (_____)

4. _____ (_____)

5. _____ (_____)

6. _____ (_____)

7. _____ (_____)

8. _____ (_____)

9. _____ (_____)

10. _____ (_____)

CHRISTMAS AROUND THE WORLD

Brazil

II A Picture Perfect Christmas

Christmas is enjoyed and celebrated in numerous ways the world over. In the frames provided illustrate **four** pictures that depict Brazilian Christmas traditions. Put a caption under each picture. Remember a picture tells a thousand words!

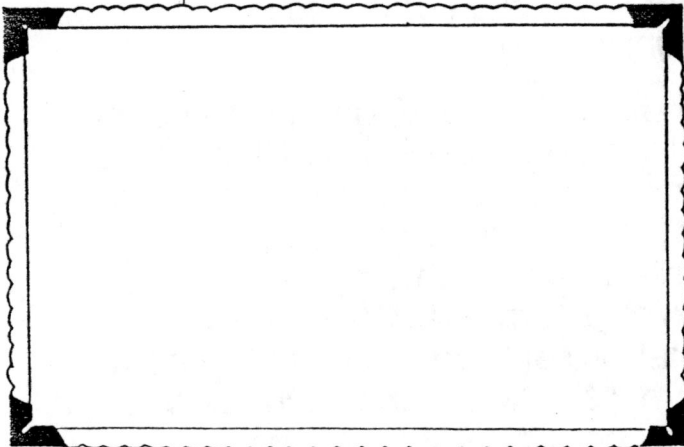

1. _____

2. _____

3. _____

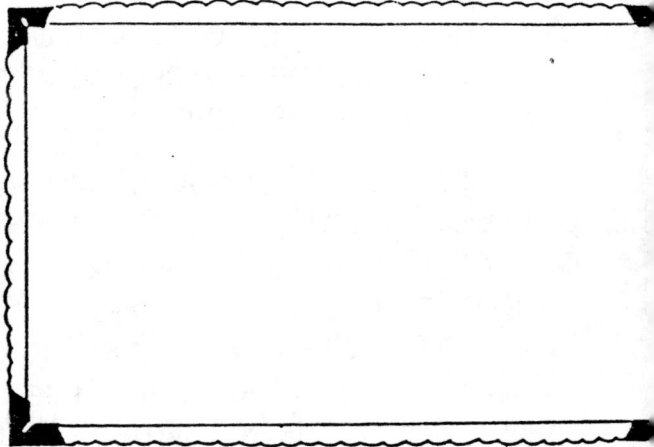

4. _____

CHRISTMAS AROUND THE WORLD

Sweden

In Sweden, the Christmas season begins on St. Lucia Day which is December the 13th. Early in the morning everyone in the house is awakened by a Lucia Bride, who is usually the oldest daughter. She dresses in a white dress with a red sash and wears a wreath of green with seven lighted candles on her head. She serves everyone else in the family coffee and buns while still in bed. She sings an old song called "Santa Lucia".

On Christmas Eve, Swedish families gather in the kitchen to take part in an old tradition called "doppa i grytan" ("dipping in the kettle"). Each one in the family dips a piece of bread into a copper kettle filled with a broth made from sausages, pork, and cornbeef. Afterwards they enjoy a smorgasbord of breads, lut-fisk (a kind of smoked fish), white sauce or gravy, ham, etc. Dinner also includes a special rice pudding called "julgrot" which has one almond hidden inside. According to tradition, good luck comes to whoever gets the almond.

Also on Christmas Eve, the living-room doors are opened to reveal the Christmas tree decorated with ornaments, garlands, and small white candles. Everyone is excited and sings carols then someone reads aloud the story of the first Christmas.

Gifts are brought by "Jultomten" a little elf-like man who takes the place of Santa Claus for Swedish children. He wears a red suit, pointed cap and long white beard, and resembles one of Santa's elves. They also leave a big bundle of oats on trees outside for birds, for no one in Sweden forgets them on Christmas Day. After the gifts from Jultomten are opened, the family passes out their own presents to everyone. Just as in the Netherlands each person writes a rhyme or jingle giving a hint as to what is in the package.

CHRISTMAS AROUND THE WORLD

On December the 25th, people go to an early church service then have a quiet restful Christmas Day. Candles are lit in the windows. On December the 26th, adults and children visit friends and relatives and eat and celebrate some more.

On January the 6th, the twelfth day after Christmas, children dress up in costumes and carry a pole with a candle covered by a paper star. They go from house to house singing and getting treats.

CHRISTMAS AROUND THE WORLD

Sweden

I The song "The Twelve Days of Christmas" refers to the twelve days between December the 25th and January the 6th. On each of the twelve days in the song, a gift was given. The twelve gifts are listed below but are not exactly as they should be. Can you rearrange them so that they are not mixed up? Then perhaps you and your classmates can sing the song together.

♪*On the twelfth day of Christmas, my true love gave to me* ♪

twelve lords a-swimming _____

eleven ladies in a pear tree _____

ten pipers dancing _____

nine drummers a-milking _____

eight maids drumming _____

seven swans a-laying _____

six geese piping _____

five gold hens _____

four calling doves _____

three French rings _____

two turtle birds _____

and a partridge a-leaping _____

Challenge: If you were to sing the song in its entirety, how many gifts would you find mentioned altogether?_____

CHRISTMAS AROUND THE WORLD

Sweden
Answers (for teachers' use only)
On the twelfth day of Christmas, my true love gave to me -

twelve lords a-leaping

eleven ladies dancing

ten pipers piping

nine drummers drumming

eight maids a-milking

seven swans a-swimming

six geese a-laying

five gold rings

four calling birds

three French hens

two turtle doves

and a partridge in a pear tree

Challenge: 364 gifts

CHRISTMAS AROUND THE WORLD

Sweden

II Valu - able Words

Give a value to all the letters of the alphabet starting with **a = #0.01,** then **B = $0.02, c = $0.03, d = $0.04, e = $0.05** up to **z = 0.26**. Find the value of the following words.

S = _____   L = _____   C = _____   T = _____   C = _____   S = _____
W = _____   U = _____   H = _____   R = _____   A = _____   M = _____
E = _____   C = _____   R = _____   A = _____   N = _____   O = _____
D = _____   I = _____   I = _____   D = _____   D = _____   R = _____
E = _____   A = _____   S = _____   I = _____   L = _____   G = _____
N = _____   [____]   T = _____   T = _____   E = _____   A = _____
     [____]   M = _____   I = _____   S = _____   S = _____
                        A = _____   O = _____   [____]   B = _____
                        S = _____   N = _____   O = _____
                            [____]   [____]   R = _____
                                                     D = _____
                                                         [____]

F = _____   W = _____   P = _____   A = _____
A = _____   R = _____   U = _____   L = _____
M = _____   E = _____   D = _____   M = _____
I = _____   A = _____   D = _____   O = _____
L = _____   T = _____   I = _____   N = _____
I = _____   H = _____   N = _____   D = _____
E = _____   [____]   G = _____   [____]
S = _____   [____]
     [____]

What is the most expensive word? _____

What is the least expensive word? _____

What is the total value of **all** the words? _____

CHRISTMAS AROUND THE WORLD

Poland

On Christmas Eve, the first star in the sky marks the beginning of the "Festival of the Star". The star represents the star of Bethlehem and it's a signal that the evening meal may begin. Prior to its appearance, the Polish people have to fast for one day. This is know as "wigilia".

Before the meal starts, small white wafers, which have scenes of the Nativity on them, are distributed to everyone. They are called peace wafers and have been blessed by the church. Family members share their peace wafers with each other as a symbol of friendship and peace on earth. The meal itself must have an even number of guests and an odd number of dishes. The meal consists of various kinds of fish, cabbage, soup, buckwheat, poppy seed rolls and so on. Meat is never served at this special supper!

In Polish homes, straw is spread on the kitchen floor and under the tablecloth to represent the stable where Jesus was born and a place setting is always put down for the Christ Child.

Once supper is completed, the "Star Man" arrives to test the children on the knowledge of their religion. He then gives the children small gifts. Along with him come three "Star Boys" who sing carols and carry a star that lights up. Prior to this, on December the 6th, the children also receive presents from Saint Nicholas.

At midnight the Polish attend Mass which is called Pasterka - the Mass of the Shepherds.

CHRISTMAS AROUND THE WORLD

Poland

I Merry Christmas

If you were celebrating Christmas in Poland one would greet you by saying "Wesolych Swiat" which means Merry Christmas. It doesn't matter how it's said, the meaning and the feeling of friendship this greeting portrays is universal.

Below are listed various ways of saying Merry Christmas in many different languages (Column A). Try to match these sayings with their appropriate countries (Column B). Use encyclopedias and other appropriate reference books to assist you. The first one is done for you.

Column A	Column B
1. Kala Christougenna <u>n</u>	(a) Russia
2. Wesolych Swiat ___	(b) Italy
3. Joyeux Noël ___	(c) The Netherlands
4. Felices Pascuas, Feliz Navidad ___	(d) Mexico, Spain
5. Froehliche Weinachten ___	(e) Japan
6. S Rozhdestvom Kristovym ___	(f) Poland
7. Sheng Dan Kuai Le ___	(g) Denmark and Norway
8. Buon Natale ___	(h) Sweden

CHRISTMAS AROUND THE WORLD

Column A	Column B

Column A

9. Zaliz Kerstfeest ___

10. Meri Kurisumasu ___

11. Gledelig Jul ___

12. God Jul ___

13. Hauskaa Joulua ___

14. Kéllemes Karácsonyi Unnepeket ___

Column B

(i) France

(j) Finland

(k) Austria and Germany

(l) China

(m) Hungary

(n) Greece

CHRISTMAS AROUND THE WORLD

Poland

II Christmas "Slides" Along

You are a Polish child and you wish to prepare a slide presentation to send to a cousin in Canada. Complete the slides given with pictures that would portray your Polish Christmas. e.g. the tree, the three Star-Men, the straw in the kitchen etc. Beside each slide write the commentary that you could later put on a tape to accompany your slide presentation.

Visual (Slides)   **Audio (words to be taped)**

CHRISTMAS AROUND THE WORLD

CHRISTMAS AROUND THE WORLD

Austria

People in Austria celebrate Christmas for one month beginning on December the 6th with the arrival of two messengers, good Saint Nicholas (Santa Klausen) and his companion Krampus who carries a rod. Austrian children tell about their good and bad deeds of the past year and promise to be very good. Saint Nicholas gives them a small sack of candies and nuts.

Christmas Eve and Christmas Day are happy times for Austrian children. They believe that the "Christkind" (Christ Child), a childlike person wearing a white robe, gold crown and wings helps to decorate the tree and also brings them presents on   Christmas Eve. On this night, the family has a special supper of fish usually carp, before the living-room   doors are unlocked and the tall lighted tree hung with sugar plums, tinsel, orna ments, and candles is revealed. "Silent Night" is sung before opening the gifts.

People carrying torches walk in procession to a special midnight service at church on Christmas Eve.

Family and friends celebrate by visiting each other on December the 25th. They feast this day on roast goose, ham, fruit cake, and cookies.

Nativity scenes and Advent Wreaths are displayed in most homes in Austria.

In Austria, over ninety percent of the people speak German. When they greet each other with season's greetings, they say "Fröhliche Weinachten!"

CHRISTMAS AROUND THE WORLD

Austria

I Compose Yourself -

Most carols sung today were originally composed in the 1700's and 1800's. "Silent Night" was written on Christmas Eve around 1818 in a little village in Austria. Joseph Mohr, a pastor in the church, discovered that the organ was broken and thought it would be a silent night. As a result of this, he wrote the words to the famous carol. Franz Gruber, the organist of Mohr's church, composed the music that same night and the carol was sung at midnight church service in Austria.

Look at the underlined words in "Silent Night". Using a dictionary or thesaurus, write words that mean the same or almost the same (synonyms). Write your new version on the lines provided. Perhaps you could write it with a partner and then sing it to the class.

Silent Night

Silent night, holy night
All is calm, all is bright
"Round yon virgin mother and child
Holy infant so tender and mild,
Sleep in heavenly peace,
Sleep in heavenly peace.

Silent night, holy night
Shepherds quake at the sight,
Glories stream from heaven afar
Heavenly hosts sing Hallelujah!
Christ the Saviour is born!
Christ the Saviour is born!

CHRISTMAS AROUND THE WORLD

Austria

Silent Night, Holy Night

_____
_____
_____
_____
_____
_____
_____
_____
_____
_____
_____
_____
_____
_____
_____

CHRISTMAS AROUND THE WORLD

Austria

II Poetry That Shapes Up -

Give your Christmas poems more meaning by writing concrete poetry. Write a poem in the shape of one of the following:

tree	candle	wreath
ornament	candy cane	bell
star		

For example: **The Christmas Tree**

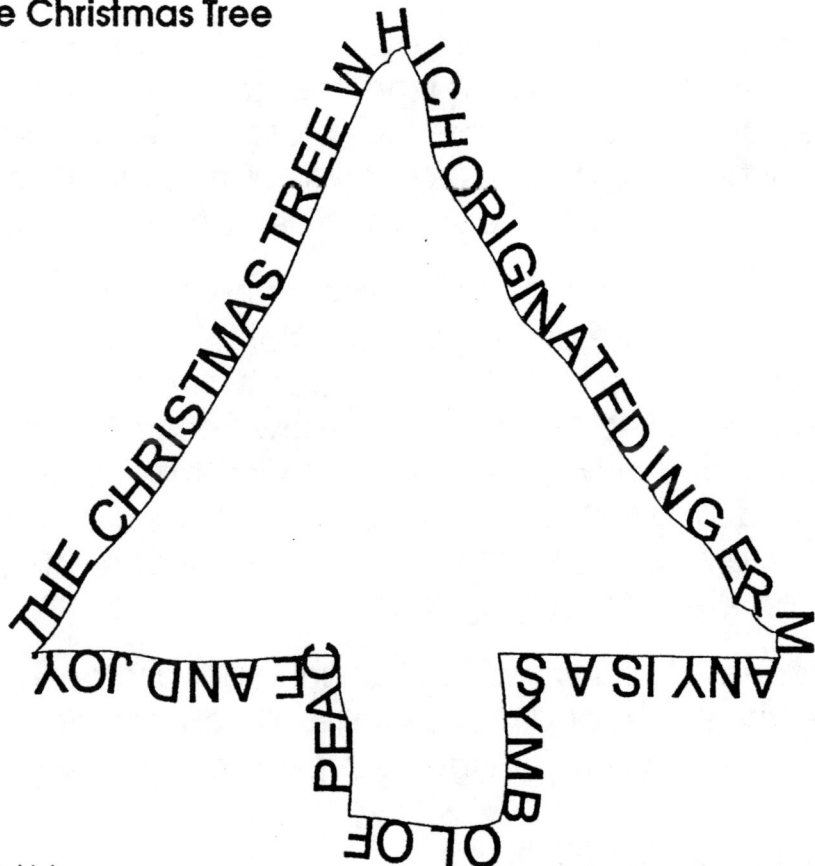

THE CHRISTMAS TREE WHICH ORIGINATED IN GERMANY IS A SYMBOL OF PEACE AND JOY

CHRISTMAS AROUND THE WORLD

Japan

Until a century ago, Christmas was not celebrated in Japan. Today it is widely acknowledged by the Christian population and even those who do not practise Christianity have grown to enjoy Christmas as a special holiday.

During the Christmas season, Japan becomes alive with festivals, some are religious and others are geared toward entertaining the children. The Japanese also enjoy presenting and viewing religious plays.

The Japanese decorate their Christmas trees with fluted paper ornaments such as fans, colourfully wrapped candy and small toys and of course, lights. Santa Claus is believed to have eyes in the back of his head so that he can carefully keep an eye on the children's behaviour to make sure that they are being good.

The Japanese manufacture a large number of products for markets all over the world. At Christmas time, the stores in Japan are a bustle of activity as people shop for Christmas presents. Festive decorations adorn the cities. One would see decorated Christmas trees, lights and feel the high spirited pulse of a society preparing to celebrate.

The most widely celebrated event of the Japanese calendar is New Year's Day. Homes are housecleaned prior to this day and decorated with bamboo, apricot and pine. On each side of the front entrance to their homes, you might find the gate pine known as kadomatsu. This particular decoration is used only at New Year's. As in other countries, special foods are prepared for a festive meal and visiting friends and relatives is popular. Many gifts are exchanged at this time. The children enjoy this holiday to the fullest - flying kites and playing games.

During these holidays, which last until January the 20th, many Japanese visit shrines and make firm resolutions for the New Year. New Year's celebrations in Japan are as important as our Christmas celebrations.

CHRISTMAS AROUND THE WORLD

Japan

I Christmas Haiku

Haiku is a type of poem that originated in Japan. The Haiku poem is unrhymed. The topics chosen are usually about nature or special times. The poems create a picture in your mind or a feeling, in your soul. They are simple but very effective.

Haiku consists of three lines:

Line one has five syllables.

Line two has seven syllables.

Line three has five syllables.

Here is an example for you:

Christmas in Japan,

Fluted ornaments on trees,

Joy and peace prevails!

Now try your hand at writing a Haiku poem about Christmas and/or New Year's celebrations in Japan.

Write your poem on the fan shape provided.

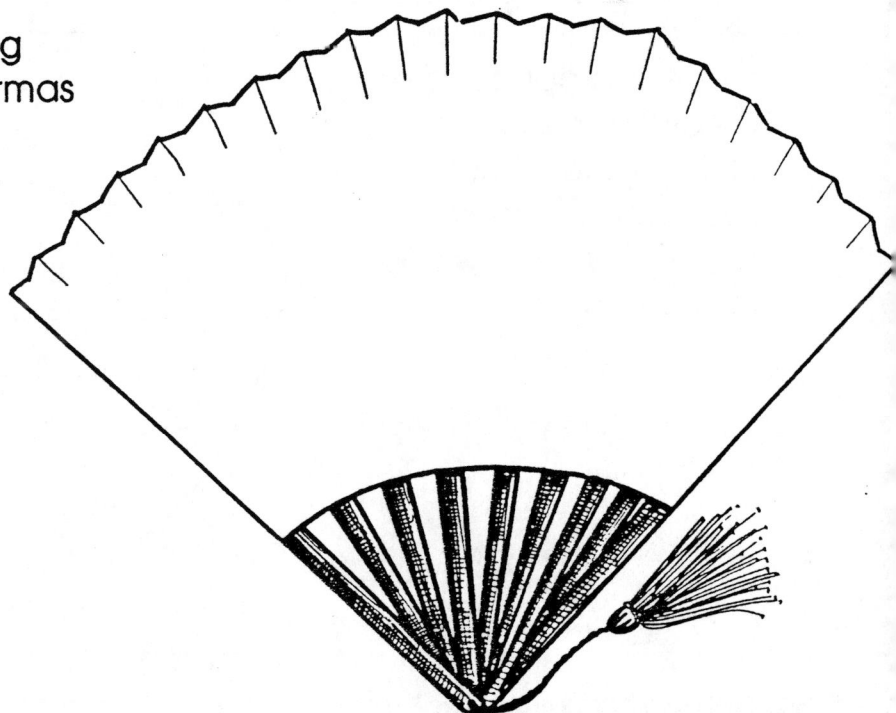

CHRISTMAS AROUND THE WORLD

Japan

II Dreams Come True

As you have learned, New Year's festivities in Japan are as important as our Christmas celebrations. The second night of New Year's is very important to the Japanese people as they believe that on this night their future is foretold in their dreams. They believe that if one dreamed about an earthquake, that meant a change of job location - a definite move was in store. If one dreamed about a ship loaded with treasure that meant prosperous days were ahead. To dream of rain meant days of anxiety or worry were to come. If one was lucky enough to dream about a sea voyage or a sun rising they could look forward to good fortune in the future.

Pretend that you believe that your dreams on Christmas Eve reveal to you a prediction about what is to come in the year ahead. Your fate, favourable or not, is prophesied on this special night. In the crystal ball provided write about your dream and what impact it will have upon your future.

CHRISTMAS AROUND THE WORLD

Italy

Do you know what a "presipio" is? It is an Italian nativity scene containing figures of baby Jesus, Mary, Joseph, the shepherds, the three kings, the angels, and the animals that came to see Baby Jesus on the first Christmas. In Italy most homes and churches have a "Presipio". The manger scene originated in Italy. Christmas lasts for three weeks from December the 18th to January the 6th.

The day before Christmas is a fast day - people do not eat any food for twenty-four hours. On Christmas Eve there is a wonderful banquet where fried, baked, or roasted eel is often the main dish served along with pastries, fruit, nuts, and "panettone" a sweet fruit bread. Before the banquet children write a Christmas letter to their parents promising to be good and after the banquet everyone in the family chooses a gift from a large crock called the "Urn of Fate". At midnight on Christmas Eve everyone goes to church services. From then until the Eve of Epiphany (December the 6th) the observance of the Yuletide in Italy is of a religious nature.

La Befana brings gifts to children on the night of January the 5th. Legend tells us that La Befana, who looks like a witch and rides a broomstick, was approached in her cottage by the Three Wise Men who requested that she come with them to help find the special baby who had been born in Bethlehem. Because she was busy doing her chores, La Befana refused. However, she realized that seeing the baby Jesus was more important than sweeping and she rushed after them with her broom in her hand. But it was too late! She never found them but while wandering from place to place, she began leaving gifts for good children and threatening naughty children with bags of ashes.

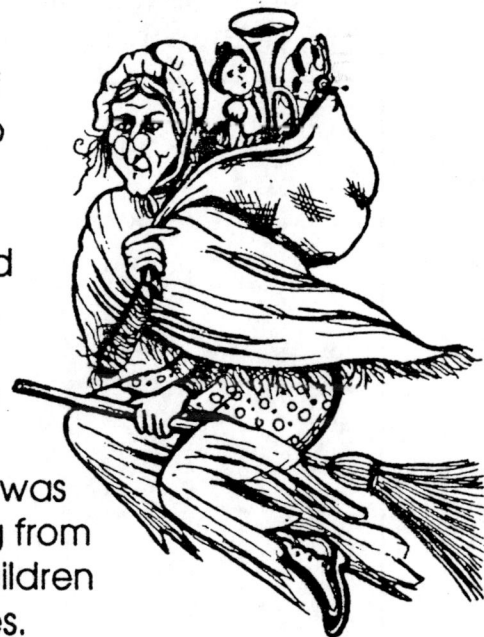

And so on the morning of January the 6th, Italian boys and girls find their stockings bulging with toys, candies and many other gifts.

CHRISTMAS AROUND THE WORLD

Italy

I A Christmas Scene in Italy -

Read the paragraph below. Write the meanings of the underlined words. Use your dictionary to help you.

Once you have a good understanding of the words, draw and colour the scene as it is described to you.

In the centre stands an <u>emerald</u> coloured house with <u>crimson</u> <u>shutters</u> on three windows. In front of an <u>azure</u> coloured door, stands a <u>charwoman</u> with a broom in her hand. She is the <u>endearing</u> witch La Befana, wearing a dress as dark as <u>ebony</u>. On her head she wears a yellow <u>kerchief</u> which is <u>dappled</u> with <u>chartreuse</u>. To the right of the house stands an <u>olive</u> <u>tree</u> <u>adorned</u> with candy canes. To the left is a garden filled with flowers of many brilliant colours - <u>violet</u>, <u>sapphire</u>, <u>ruby</u>, yellow and orange.

CHRISTMAS AROUND THE WORLD

Italy

II "Toy" with Creative Writing -

Games, stuffed animals, trains, dolls and numerous other toys crowd store shelves at Christmas time. Everyone loves toys but what do we know about them? The first jack-in-the-box made in 1752 was actually a bird in the box which sang when the top was lifted. Dolls have not always been playthings. In ancient times they were thought to carry spirits. Toy soldiers became stocking stuffers as a result of war victories by Frederick the Great, King of Prussia. The hobbyhorse is one of the oldest toys seen in a fifteenth century painting.

No matter what the toy is, or who the gift giver is, or where children live, every child looks forward with excitement each Christmas morning to look at their new toys.

Choose <u>one</u> of the following titles and write a creative story about toys. Perhaps you could make it amusing.

The Last Toy on the Shelf	**The Night It Rained Toys**
Toys Alive!	**The North Pole Toy Mystery**
The Toy Machine	**Toys - The Night After Christmas**
Lost in the Toy Department	**The Magical Toy**
Oops... The Wrong Toy	**Last Year's Toys**

Italy

CHRISTMAS AROUND THE WORLD

Norway

Christmas customs in Norway had their start a long time ago. One traditional custom actually begins late in the autumn during harvest time. The Norwegian people put aside the best of their wheat and when Christmas time comes they put the sheaves of wheat on poles which they make from tree branches. These provide an excellent spot for birds to perch. The Norwegians clear away a circular area underneath the poles. Here they believe the birds play and dance working up an appetite for their next meal.

Prior to sunset on Christmas Eve, the wheat in the yard is checked and if there are numerous sparrows indulging in a meal the Norwegians believe that this means that they will have a good year for growing crops. After checking out the sparrows, the family enjoys a big, delicious dinner of favourite dishes. Once dinner is complete everyone opens their gifts.

Before going to bed, the Norwegians make preparations to ward off the mischievous spirits and witches that their ancestors long ago used to feel came out on Christmas Eve. This custom has been maintained throughout the years. The people continue to hide their brooms so the witches won't play with them. A fire is also lit in the fireplace to prevent the witches from coming down the chimney. They are also careful to leave lamps burning throughout the entire night to keep these spirits at bay. A single bright light is always put in a front window as a welcome to friends.

On Christmas Day, families get ready to go to church. Afterwards they share a quiet, family day at home - a cosy day filled with joy and warmth.

CHRISTMAS AROUND THE WORLD

Norway

I Customs - New and Old

Customs are different the world over. As you have read one Norwegian custom is to put sheaves of wheat on poles or fences for the birds to feed upon. I'm sure your family has its own special traditions too. In the space provided write about some of your very own Christmas traditions or customs. Tell which ones are your favourites or if any have been passed down from past generations. Which ones are new - invented solely by your own family? Which customs will you be sure to share with your own children when you are an adult?

My Christmas Traditions

CHRISTMAS AROUND THE WORLD

Norway

II Which Witch is Which?

Homonyms are words that sound alike but have different spellings and different meanings. The homonyms in the boxes below were taken from the information on Christmas in Norway. Fill in the missing words. Then give the meaning for each on the lines provided. The first one is done for you.

A

1. witch   one who has supernatural powers especially to work evil

2. which   a thing designated e.g. the story which we preferred

1. their
2. _____
3. _____

1. night
2. _____

CHRISTMAS AROUND THE WORLD

1. time
2. _____ _____

_____

1. one
2. _____ _____

_____

1. to
2. _____ _____

_____

B Prove your understanding of the meaning of the above words by writing each one in a "Christmas"-y sentence. Use variety in your sentences.

CHRISTMAS AROUND THE WORLD

Denmark

Santa Claus is a familiar figure in the Scandinavian countries of Norway, Sweden, and Denmark. Many children there believe that a lively elf brings them gifts from Santa on Christmas Eve. The Danes and Norwegians call this elf "Julenissen". He is dressed in a grey suit, red bonnet, has a long white beard, and wears red stockings and white clogs. He is married and has several children all of whom wear red caps.

Christmas Eve dinner begins with a rice pudding called "julgröt" which has an almond in it. Whoever gets the almond wins a surprise. Dinner continues with roast goose stuffed with apples and prunes, served with potatoes, cabbage, cake, pastries, and other baked goods.

In Denmark people decorate their trees with small paper cones filled with candy as well as hearts, bells, and candles. Children are not allowed to see the tree until Christmas Eve. After dinner, the candles are lit, hymns are sung, and gifts are passed out.

In Denmark birds are fed well with suet, bread and grain. People believe that if a lot of birds come to eat the food which is placed in the yards of farms and houses, that good crops will come to the farm.

Traditionally a large bonfire is usually built outdoors. Candles in the home are lit representing light, friendship and warmth. Candles are lit in the windows welcoming strangers or travellers into the home for food or shelter.

In Denmark another tradition that is popular is the hanging of plates on walls in homes. This tradition began when Christmas cookies were given on beautiful plates to servants at Christmas time. The servants afterwards hung the plates on the walls.

CHRISTMAS AROUND THE WORLD

Denmark

I (a) What is your favourite Christmas tradition?

_____

_____

(b) What is your favourite Christmas meal?

_____

_____

_____

(c) What Christmas decorations are put up every December in your house?

_____

_____

_____

(d) What are two of your favourite Christmas carols?

_____

_____

(e) Decorate the house that follows with your favourite decorations. Perhaps you will want to include such things as strings of colourful lights, candles in the window, Christmas tree in the window, wreath on the door, etc.

CHRISTMAS AROUND THE WORLD

CHRISTMAS AROUND THE WORLD

Denmark

II The Christmas stamp was invented in Denmark by a Danish postmaster. All profits from the sale of the stamp were and still are given to charity.

If **you** had the opportunity to design a Christmas stamp to be used for the month of December where you live, what would you like to see on it? Perhaps some day a philatelist would like to have it in his collection!

CHRISTMAS AROUND THE WORLD

Denmark

III Elves are imaginary creatures often found in folk tales of Denmark and other Northern European counties. They are most often portrayed as tiny, happy people who possess magical powers, often bringing good luck to humans. Have you read the fairy tale called "The Elves and the Shoemaker"? Elves are also known as fairies. Below are other names by which elf-like creatures are known in different parts of the world. The letters in the names have been scrambled. You must get to work and spell them correctly. Good Luck!

1. ogmen _____

2. exiip _____

3. renbowi _____

4. inglob _____

5. lrolt _____

6. phelcrunae _____

7. frawd _____

What is the traditional role of the elf as we know it at Christmas time?

_____

_____

What is the role of the elf in Denmark?

_____

_____

CHRISTMAS AROUND THE WORLD

Greece

Many times we see "Xmas" written as an abbreviated form for Christmas. Have you ever wondered where the "X" came from? This tradition originated in Greece long ago during the time of the early Christian church. In the Greek language, "X" is the first letter of Christ's name. Consequently Xmas was frequently used and has been ever since this time.

Christmas carols are popular in Greece as in most countries of the world. The actual word "carol" comes from a dance popular in Greece known as the "chorauliein". This dance was once accompanied by flute music. Later this dance spread among the countries of Europe. The French, in particular, adopted this dance but instead of flute music, they would sing. Before long the word "carol" became associated with song rather than dance. At first carols were sung at special events but as time went on they were solely associated with Christmas time.

One traditional Greek belief is quite unusual. The Greek people must try to be very good during the Christmas season but especially on Christmas Eve when Kallikantzaroi are on the rounds, roaming about the country. These Kallikantzaroi are considered to be monsters, with gigantic heads and bodies covered with hair. They break into homes and do many mischievous things. They also gobble up all the food that was prepared for Christmas and even destroy the furniture. As a ploy to keep them away from their Christmas delicacies, the Greek people hang sausages and sweets in the fireplace with the hope that the monsters will eat these instead. If all their attempts to rid themselves of the monsters fail, they then resort to having a priest come to bless the house and scare the Kallikantzaroi away.

CHRISTMAS AROUND THE WORLD

Greece

I The Custom of the Christmas Stocking

"The stockings were hung by the chimney with care..." The custom of hanging stockings on Christmas Eve comes from an old Greek legend. It is said that Saint Nicholas, who was believed to be a kind prominent Greek bishop, felt sorry for a poor man whose three daughters could not get married because the man had no gold for their dowries. One night, hidden by the guise of darkness, the bishop went to the man's house and dropped some gold down his chimney. By accident the gold landed in one of the oldest daughter's stockings that she had hung by the fire to dry. The next morning the daughter found the treasure and was elated that she could now get married.

The other two daughters each took their turn hanging up their stockings surmising that St. Nicholas would return with more gold. They went to bed with anticipation in their hearts. Their wishes came true and all the girls were able to get married. The news spread. As time went on children started to hang their stockings on the fireplace hoping to find a surprise in them in the morning. Thus the custom of the Christmas stocking was born!

A On the stockings provided are words taken from this legend. Find each word in your dictionary and write its meaning on the line.

CHRISTMAS AROUND THE WORLD

1. prominent

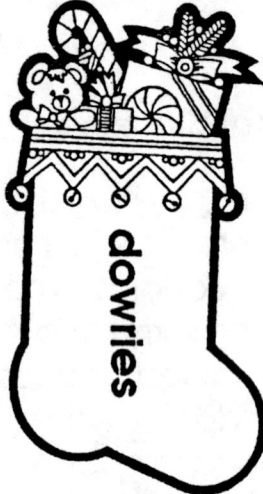

2. dowries

3. elated

4. anticipation

5. surmising

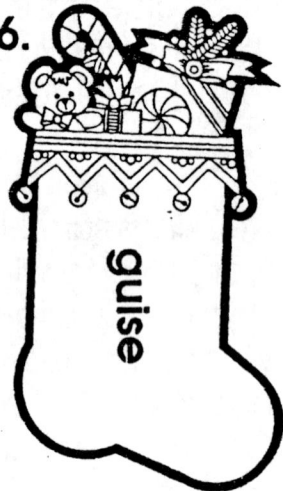

6. guise

1. _____

2. _____

3. _____

4. _____

5. _____

6. _____

B Now try your hand at writing your own legend about how the custom of the Christmas Stocking began.

_____

_____

_____

_____

_____

_____

_____

_____

_____

_____

_____

_____

_____

_____

_____

_____

_____

CHRISTMAS AROUND THE WORLD

Greece

II Christmas "Monsters"-osities

Spending Christmas with friends from Greece was an experience you'll not soon forget. Kallikantzaroi litterly bombarded the household where you stayed. The monsters were grotesque, outlandish and horrifying as they scurried about like whirling dervishes. At last they are gone and you want to write to a friend to tell about your unusual Christmas holiday. However, you've seen so much that words alone could not convey the true picture. You decide to express yourself artistically first, before you tackle your letter.

A On the easel below illustrate everything you've witnessed on the night the Kallikantzaroi attacked! Make your picture detailed, colourful and be sure to include several of these monsters as well as the destruction they caused.

CHRISTMAS AROUND THE WORLD

B Now write your letter to your friend. Use descriptive words to to relate all about your experience with Christmas "Monster"-osities.

Heading:

_____
Your street address

_____
Your city, province (state), area code (zip code)

_____
Today's date

Greeting:

_____

Body:

_____

_____

_____

_____

_____

_____

_____

Closing: _____

Signature: _____

CHRISTMAS AROUND THE WORLD

Mexico and Spain

Christmas is a very joyous time in Mexico as many celebrate the birth of Jesus. Celebrations begin in mid December. One such celebration is known as "posada" which means "resting place". A posada means a procession or a parade. It refers to the search that Joseph and Mary had when they arrived in Bethlehem - with no place to stay. As legend goes, the search for shelter went on for nine days. Nine days prior to Christmas people gather in the streets to form a posada. Many are dressed in costume; some as shepherds, others as kings and still more are disguised as an animal such as a sheep. At the front of the procession are the children who carry figures of Mary and Joseph. The group parade the streets looking for a dwelling place just as Mary and Joseph did. At last people in one of the homes allows everyone to enter. The figures of Mary and Joseph are immediately put in a very special place. These posadas go on night after night until Christmas Eve. On this night a figure of baby Jesus is also taken on the posada to be placed with the figures of Mary and Joseph. This last posada ends with a splendid Christmas party. There is a multitude of good things to eat as well as pinatas for the children and lots of laughter, music and fun.

Once the celebration nears its end, everyone gets ready to go to church. Following church there is dancing, singing and festive celebrations everywhere. The streets are aglow with candles, lanterns and electric lights. It is indeed a festive holiday season!

The pinata mentioned above, is the most famous Mexican tradition. A shape of a bird or an animal is molded from clay or paper maché. This figure is decorated with colourful tissue paper or painted in brighter colours. While making the pinata they fill it with candies, nuts or small toys. The pinata is usually suspended from the ceiling

CHRISTMAS AROUND THE WORLD

Mexico and Spain

and the children blindfolded, take turns hitting at it with a stick until it breaks apart and the treasures scatter all over the place. The children, shrieking with joy, scamper to gather the treats.

Christmas celebrations and customs in Spain are very much the same as those of Mexico. The town square is the centre of activity. The children have a wonderful time on the swings which are set up. They say that their swinging helps the Sun, which they refer to as "Sol", move along to warm other places. During the season of Christmas, Sol starts its journey to the north and the children want to help Sol bring its glorious sunshine to their northern neighbours in other countries.

The people of Spain celebrate with great joy on Christmas Eve as they dance and sing in the streets. In almost every Spanish home one would find a nativity scene known as "Nacimiento". On Christmas morning the people usually go to church and then spend the rest of the day with the family and close friends. On Christmas night, it is customary, in Spain, to go to the village square where they will find the "urn of fate". Everyone writes their name on a piece of paper and puts it into the urn. Afterwards names are drawn out two at a time and that couple vow to be best friends for the upcoming new year.

On the Twelfth Night, January the 6th, Spanish children make sure that they put their shoes near a window or a door. In them they put barley. In the morning their shoes are filled with candy and gifts left by the Wise Men. The barley is gone, as it is eaten by the Wise Men's camels. This day known as the Epiphany, marks the last day of the Christmas season.

CHRISTMAS AROUND THE WORLD

Mexico and Spain

I Capitalizing on the Poinsettia

A Rewrite the paragraph about how the poinsettia became a popular Christmas flower. Put in all necessary capitals and punctuation.

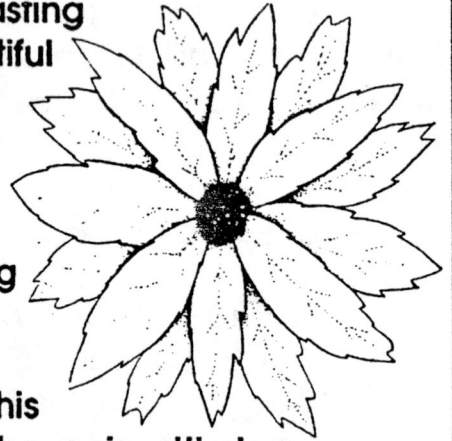

the brilliant red or stark white flowers and contrasting deep green leaves make the poinsettia a beautiful christmas flower this gorgeous plant is native to mexico as legend goes a long time ago a boy named pablo desired to give a gift to jesus mother mary pablo searched but could find nothing to take to mary so he settled on bringing her a bouquet of weeds as he passed these weeds to mary they instantaneously turned into beautiful star-shaped flowers scarlet in colour this was the very first poinsettia ever since this day the poinsettia has been associated with christmas

B Now that you know the legend of the poinsettia, do some research and see if you can find out why each of the following are associated with Christmas.

(a) holly

(b) mistletoe

CHRISTMAS AROUND THE WORLD

Mexico and Spain

II My Very Own Posada

You are planning on having a very special Christmas party but to make it a little more interesting you decide to have a Mexican posada. You're sure this will be a real hit with your friends. You have many preparations to consider and a few changes perhaps are in store to make things more to your liking.

What parts of the posada would you change or omit?
What parts would definitely stay?
Your friends are perhaps unaware of what a posada is; therefore you must put a note in each invitation describing the events - the procession, costumes etc.
You must also plan the party.
What food will you serve?
What shape will your pinata be and what will you fill it with?
Your excitement escalates as you think about how much fun this will be.

A Below write a description of what a posada is in your own words. Be careful of spelling and punctuation. Use the back of this sheet too.

_____

_____

_____

_____

_____

_____

_____

_____

_____

B Complete your invitation to your Christmas posada.
Remember to mention the time, place etc.

An Invitation

_____
_____
_____
_____
_____
_____
_____
_____
_____
_____
_____
_____
_____
_____
_____

WELCOME

CHRISTMAS AROUND THE WORLD

France

Large numbers of French families decorate their homes with Nativity scenes. In France, a nativity scene is called a crèche. In these scenes are "santons", clay figures which depict the story of the birth of the baby Jesus. Figures of the Magi, angels, shepherds, and various animals surround the Holy Family.

A few days before Christmas, the Christmas tree is decorated with candles, stars, lights, and tinsel. Children put their shoes in front of the fireplace to be filled with gifts by Père Noël (Father Christmas). In olden days, French children would leave their "sabots", wooden shoes, by the fireside to be filled. While children sleep, Père Noël fills the little shoes and on Christmas morning, everyone gets together to exchange and open presents.

Many families attend Midnight Mass and afterwards have a festive dinner called "Le réveillon". These dinners may include goose or turkey, buckwheat cakes with sour cream, oysters, chestnuts, fruit, and a Christmas cake called "bûche de Noël", which is made in the shape of a Yule Log.

Christmas plays and puppet shows are enjoyed by many families.

"O Holy Night", a famous Christmas carol, was introduced at Midnight Mass in 1847. A French composer, Adolphe Adam, wrote the music.

CHRISTMAS AROUND THE WORLD

France

I Today Santa Claus brings presents to children in many countries, including Canada, the United States and Australia. Other countries have their own version of Santa Claus such as Père Noël in France. Your job is to track down Santa Claus in several other countries which are listed below and try and find out what Santa is known as there.

Country	Name
1. Canada, U.S.A., Australia	Santa Claus
2. France	Père Noël
3. Germany	_____
4. Britain	_____
5. Italy	_____
6. Sweden	_____
7. The Netherlands	_____
8. Brazil	_____
9. Commonwealth of Independent States	_____
10. Switzerland	_____

II Reread the information given about Christmas in France. Try to determine what the following French words mean:

1. Le réveillon _____

2. crèche _____

CHRISTMAS AROUND THE WORLD

3. bûche de Noël _____

4. santons _____

5. Père Noël _____

6. sabots _____

7. Joyeux Noël _____

III Write a paragraph describing a favourite Christmas memory. You might want to write about your earliest Christmas memory, the best part of Christmas, or your favourite Christmas gift ever.

Illustrate your paragraph.

CHRISTMAS AROUND THE WORLD

Commonwealth of Independent States (C.I.S.)

(Formerly U.S.S.R.)

People in the C.I.S. (Commonwealth of Independent States) celebrate Christmas enthusiastically. In the city of Leningrad, in particular, people make the holiday into a midwinter festival which includes many exciting and special events for children. The people have adopted many foreign Christmas customs such as great feasts of roast goose and plum pudding from England, beautifully decorated Christmas trees, a tradition which originated in Germany, and presents from a female Santa known as Grandmother Babushka.

Leningrad offers its children another special pleasure for Christmas. Parents traditionally take their children to see a large spectacular production put on by the ballet company which children find quite magical - the very scenery transforms itself into something completely different in front of their eyes. Many talented people must work hard to make a good ballet. These include dancers, musicians, designers, stagehands, choreographers, and composers.

The first Russian composer to gain international fame was Peter Ilich Tchaikovsky (1840-1893), born in Votkinsk. Tchaikovsky's three ballets have become classics. They are "Swan Lake" (1875-1876), "Sleeping Beauty" (1888-1889), and the "Nutcracker" which had its first performance in December, 1892 (almost one hundred years ago!)

CHRISTMAS AROUND THE WORLD

Commonwealth of Independent States (C.I.S.)

I Read the following sentences which tell the story of "The Nutcracker". The sentences contain many action words (verbs) which have words ending in ly telling "how" the action is carried out (adverbs).

For example:

On Christmas Eve, Herr Drosselmeyer, an inventor, brought the children Fritz and Clara, a set of dolls that danced mechanically up and down the living-room.

In this sentence **danced** is the action word (verb) and **mechanically** tells "how" (adverb) the dolls danced.

Read the twelve sentences carefully to determine the action words with their adverbs and list them in the chart.

1. The inventor produced a nutcracker shaped like a soldier wearing a bright uniform, and then he broke a nut sharply between its jaws.

2. Fritz carelessly cracked a large nut with the nutcracker and the jaws split in half.

3. Clara carefully tucked the nutcracker into her doll's bed under the tree before going upstairs to bed.

4. She could not sleep, however, so crept cautiously downstairs and entered the dark living-room as the clock struck twelve.

5. Suddenly she noticed that the Christmas tree was glowing and the lights twinkled in the darkness.

6. Thinking that she was dreaming, Clara hid behind a chair and watched as mice began to gnaw hungrily at the sugar plums and other decorations.

CHRISTMAS AROUND THE WORLD

Commonwealth of Independent States (C.I.S.)

7. The soldiers came alive and led by the nutcracker, they bitterly fought the mice. Clara threw her slipper and killed the Mouse King.

8. The Nutcracker then turned into a handsome Prince and bowed graciously to Clara.

9. Then the Nutcracker Prince and Clara magically journeyed on a sleigh made of snowflakes to meet the Sugar Plum Fairy in the Kingdom of Sweets.

10. The Sugar Plum Fairy smiled sweetly and thanked Clara kindly for all she had done as she delicately stepped onto the floor and spun on her toes to begin the most beautiful of dances.

11. Then the Nutcracker Prince danced gracefully with Clara.

12. She then opened her eyes and thought to herself, "I must have been dreaming" as she looked down at the nutcracker still tucked safely in her doll's bed.

Verbs	Adverbs
1. _____	_____
2. _____	_____
3. _____	_____
4. _____	_____
5. _____	_____

CHRISTMAS AROUND THE WORLD

Commonwealth of Independent States (C.I.S.)

Verbs	Adverbs
6. _____	_____
7. _____	_____
8. _____	_____
9. _____	_____
10. _____	_____
11. _____	_____
12. _____	_____

CHRISTMAS AROUND THE WORLD

Commonwealth of Independent States (C.I.S.)

II Characters in Stories and Songs -

There are several familiar Christmas stories and songs that traditionally have become favourites over the years. See if you can identify some of the characters associated with these Christmas favourites from the clues given below. The first one is done for you.

1. The object that magically came to life in a ballet written by the Russian composer Peter Ilich Tchaikovsky. the Nutcracker

2. The character in a famous Dr. Seus book - the one who stole Christmas! _____

3. The old miser in "A Christmas Carol" by Charles Dickens, who is famous for saying, "Bah, humbug!" _____

4. In the Bible, it is who the shepherds came to see in the manger.

   _____

5. The best selling record of all time is "White Christmas" sung by this famous singer. _____

6. The second most valuable copyright in the world sung first by Gene Autry in 1948, is about a famous reindeer who led Santa through snow and fog with his nose. _____

CHRISTMAS AROUND THE WORLD

7. In the Bible, three significant people who brought gifts to the Baby Jesus. _____

8. According to a particular song, he's the most famous snowman of all time. _____

9. Children around the world call him by different names. He is kept busy in his workshop helping elves make toys for children at Christmas time. _____

CHRISTMAS AROUND THE WORLD

Canada, the United States and Great Britain

People of all nationalities have settled in Canada and the United States. With them these immigrants brought all their Christmas traditions and customs. These customs are many and varied. People from Great Britain celebrate Christmas in much the same way as Canadians and Americans.

It is common for people to begin celebrations early in December. There are house parties and often people organize a carol sing. Those invited go from home to home singing Christmas carols. Sometimes the grateful listeners give a treat or a hot drink, such as cocoa, as a way of thanking the carollers for spreading the Christmas spirit.

The traditional Christmas meal requires much preparation. There might be roast turkey with stuffing, cranberry sauce, white or sweet potatoes, green and red jellied salads, a variety of vegetable dishes and perhaps mincemeat pie or plum pudding for dessert. Each family has their own special ethnic dishes as well. In Great Britain one might enjoy roasted goose and raise a glass of wassail in a toast. Wassail is a type of wine or ale which is spiced with cinnamon, cloves, sugar, and apples.

Tree decorating is great fun and it usually involves the whole family. The most popular trees are fir and pine although many people now use artificial trees. It is up to the individual families as to what the most appropriate time is to decorate the tree. Some are decorated very early in December while others are decorated sometime during the last week before Christmas. Decorations are generally in abundance - tinsel, ornaments of all kinds - glass bulbs, figurines of animals, angels and so on. The electric lights on the tree bring it to life.

CHRISTMAS AROUND THE WORLD

Canada, the United States and Great Britain

Some cities and towns have tree lighting ceremonies in outdoor commercial areas to officially mark the beginning of the Christmas season. Homes are festively adorned with decorative wreaths on doors and outdoor manger scenes and many, many lights. Inside one might find holly, mistletoe, poinsettias, manger scenes and Advent wreaths.

Children busy themselves writing letters to Santa Claus telling him what they would like to get for Christmas and often they assure him about how good they've been. They mail their letters to the North Pole. Stockings are also hung on the fireplace in anticipation that Santa will leave a few treasures in them.

In Great Britain the children write letters to Father Christmas (or Santa Claus) asking him for some special presents. They throw their letters into the fireplace and hope that the ashes that go up the chimney get to Santa in a magic way. The children either hang their stockings on the fireplace or at the end of their beds.

Christmas Eve, December the 24th, is very special. Santa Claus comes on that night once everyone is fast asleep. He comes on a sleigh pulled by eight reindeer and lands on the roof of each house. He tries to go down the chimney, but if it's a tight fit, he uses the front door which is left unlocked for him to enter. Santa Claus fills the stockings and leaves gifts under the tree. Very often a delicious snack of milk and cookies are left for him. Some children also leave carrots for the reindeer. The only difference between Santa Claus and Father Christmas is their appearance. Father Christmas wears a long, red robe.

CHRISTMAS AROUND THE WORLD

Canada, the United States and Great Britain

I Festive Words

In Column **A** are listed many Christmas words that are commonly heard at Christmas time in Canada, the United States and Great Britain. In Column **B** put this list of words in **ABC order**. In Column **C** show the **plural form** of each word.

The first one has been done for you.

Column A	Column B	Column C
1. present	bell	bells
2. cranberry sauce		
3. manger		
4. shepherd		
5. king		
6. candle		
7. mistletoe		
8. pine cone		
9. bell		
10. star		
11. ornament		

CHRISTMAS AROUND THE WORLD

Canada, the United States and Great Britain

Column A	Column B	Column C
12. reindeer	_____	_____
13. sleigh	_____	_____
14. candy cane	_____	_____
15. holly	_____	_____
16. poinsettia	_____	_____
17. wreath	_____	_____
18. decoration	_____	_____

B Now use as many of these words as possible in a Christmas story. Your story can be humorous, heart-warming, suspenseful or mysterious.

Some suggested titles

1. Santa Is Stuck in the Chimney!

2. The Figurine in the Manger is Alive!

3. No, Joey, Don't Eat the Poinsettia!

4. Rudolph to the Rescue

5. A title of your own choosing.

CHRISTMAS AROUND THE WORLD

Canada, the United States and Great Britain

II The First Christmas Card

Over a hundred years, in 1843, a man by the name of Henry Cole was distressed by the fact that he had no time to write letters to his friends at Christmas time. Consequently, he hired John Calcott Horsley who was an English artist, to design a card for him. Horsley designed a card which looked very similar to a postcard and it pictured a large family celebrating Christmas. Cole ordered one thousand of these cards. A man by the name of Joseph Cundall coloured each card by hand. Mr. Cundall owned a shop in England and he sold all the cards that Mr. Cole had not used. The price of the cards was very high but the idea of sending Christmas cards had been born. Soon the custom spread throughout Great Britain and as time went on it became popular the world over. In 1875 the first Christmas cards in the United States were manufactured.

Sometimes contests were held to find new and original designs for Christmas cards. A printer from Boston, Louis Prang, held these contests yearly. Pretend you decide to enter a Christmas card contest. You are determined to have a winning entry. Cut and fold the paper provided to make your card. Design an attractive cover and write a Christmas message on the inside.

III Rudolph's Relatives

No wonder Santa chose the reindeer to help him deliver toys on Christmas Eve! A single reindeer can pull a sleigh weighing 136 kg (300 pounds) They do this in parts of Northern Europe - Norway, Sweden and Finland - where Lapps follow herds of reindeer and train them as pack animals and to pull sleds and sleighs. When Lapps get together they sometimes have reindeer races for fun. Reindeer seem to fly as they run fast over the snow because their large wide hoofs prevent them from sinking.

Canada, the United States and Great Britain

Cut and fold to make a card

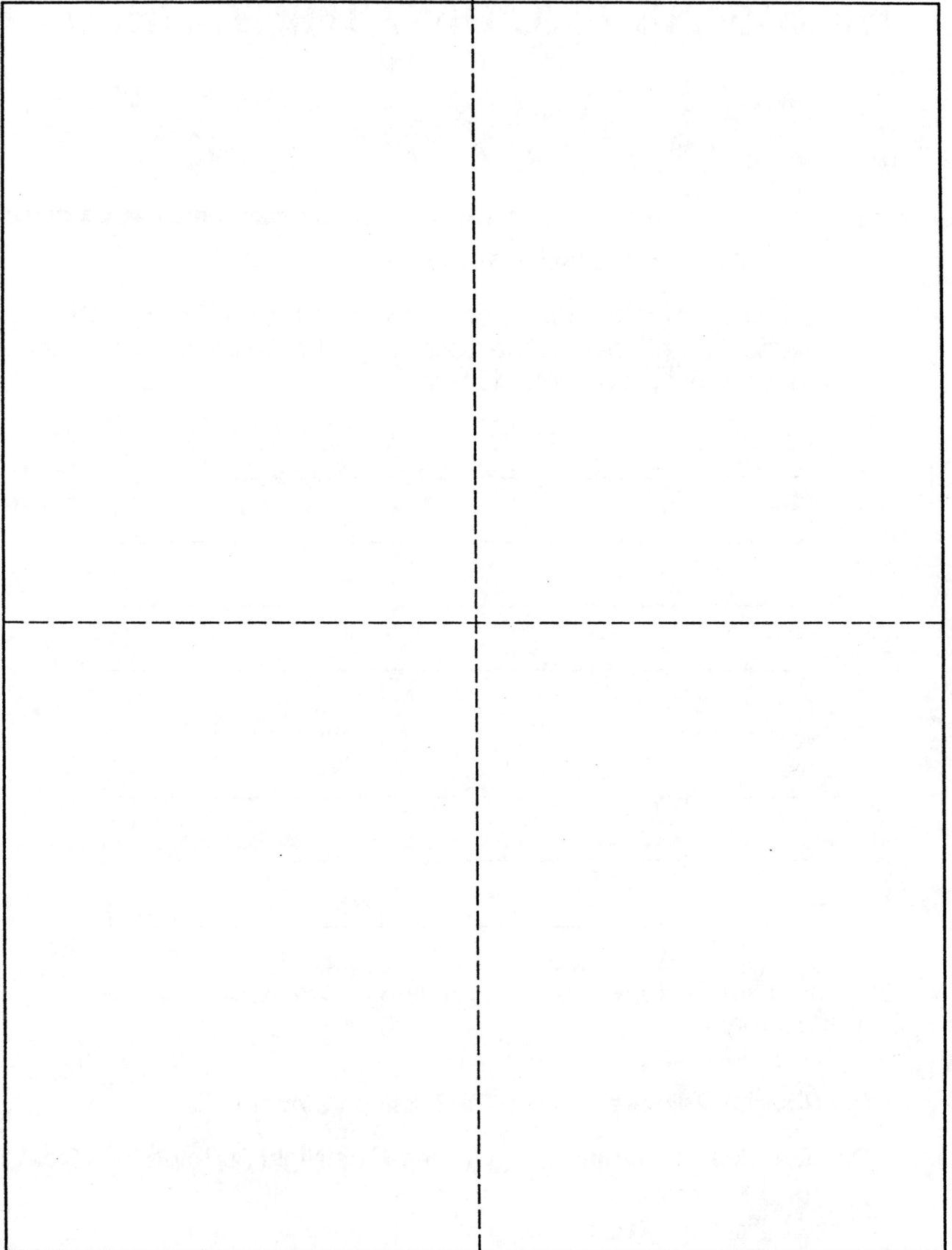

CHRISTMAS AROUND THE WORLD

Canada, the United States and Great Britain

A Search around to find the names of Santa's eight reindeer, other than Rudolph, and list them below. The beginning letter is given to help you out. Try to write them in alphabetical order.

B _____

C _____

C _____

D _____

D _____

D _____

P _____

V _____

B Choose one of the following reindeer titles and write an interesting Christmas story.

The Naughty Reindeer   **The Missing Reindeer**

One Reindeer Too Many   **Oh Deer! The Night Rudolph Was Sick**

Fogged In

CHRISTMAS AROUND THE WORLD

Canada, the United States and Great Britain

IV Christmas Classics

Over one hundred and fifty years ago, a man by the name of Dr. Clement Moore wrote the most famous of all Christmas poems - "A Visit From St. Nicholas". You may refer to it as "The Night Before Christmas". Whatever, this traditional Christmas favourite never loses its appeal and charm and it is read aloud in numerous homes all over the world on Christmas Eve. Moore was an American scholar and it is said that he wrote this poem to give to his children as a Christmas present. The poem was published in the TOY SENTINEL in New York on December 23, 1823. The author not considering his poem to be extremely good, would not sign his name to it. Such humility should be admired! The prosperity of the poem quickly spread and, to this day and for centuries to come, it will remain a classic.

Moore's beautiful Christmas poem is alive with descriptions so clear that one can picture the scenes in one's mind. It is a delight for the children whose imaginations capture these images he reveals to treasure for evermore!

Read the classic poem and then complete the following:

(a) Use your dictionary to find the meaning of each word as it pertains to the poem.

1. nestled _____

2. sash _____

3. coursers _____

4. obstacle_____

5. prancing _____

CHRISTMAS AROUND THE WORLD

CHRISTMAS AROUND THE WORLD

6. bound _____

7. tarnished _____

8. peddler _____

9. droll _____

10. thistle _____

(b) Moore describes Santa in detail. Tell what he says about each of Santa's features listed below.

1. eyes _____

2. dimples _____

3. cheeks _____

4. nose _____

5. mouth _____

6. beard _____

7. belly _____

(c) Illustrate your favourite part of "A Visit From St. Nicholas".

CHRISTMAS AROUND THE WORLD

Canada, the United States and Great Britain

(d) There are various other Christmas classics that have captured our hearts and have become as much a part of Christmas as the gift giving itself. There are great minds responsible for these masterpieces. Some of these writers are from the United States and Great Britain and yet others are from other countries.

Do some research to find out what each of the people listed below has contributed to classical Christmas literature. Then select one of the authors, read his work and prepare a one page report telling about what the story or tale was about.

Authors	Title of His Work
1. Charles Dickens	_____
2. Francis Pharcellus Church	_____
3. O. Henry	_____
4. Hans Christian Anderson	_____

CHRISTMAS AROUND THE WORLD

Canada, the United States and Great Britain

V Christmas Customs Around the World

Once December arrives there's only one thing on everybody's mind - the sights, the smells and the sounds of Christmas! Customs and traditions handed down through generations begin to come alive. Some families set up an Advent Calendar, or make an Advent wreath while others take out their treasured Star of Seven or watch a Yule log blazing on the hearth. In the interlocking circles compare your customs and traditions with those of one of the countries you've learned about. Are any of your customs the same?

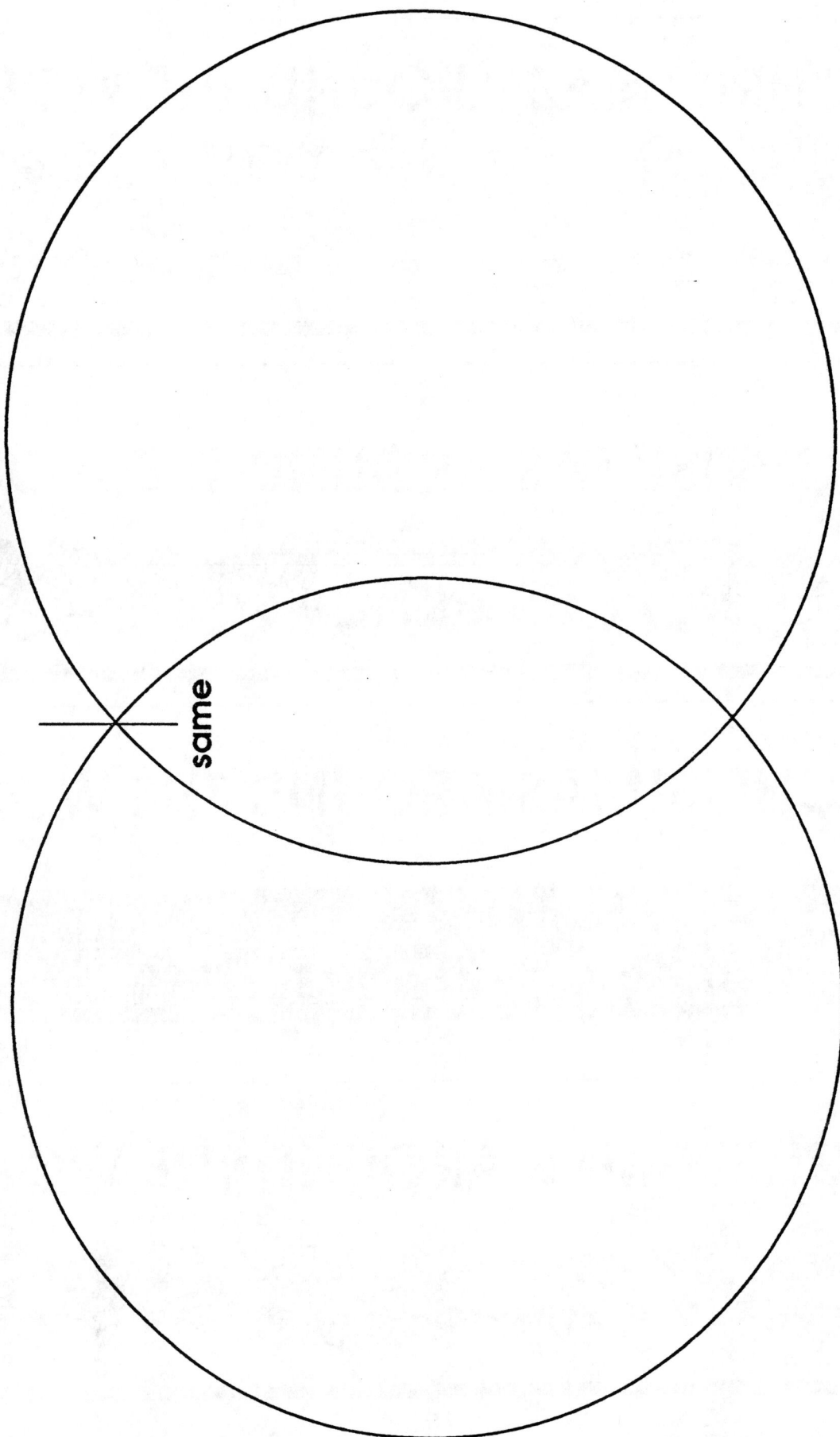

Christmas Customs

Another Country -

Your Country -

same

CHRISTMAS AROUND THE WORLD

CHRISTMAS AROUND THE WORLD

CHRISTMAS AROUND THE WORLD

CHRISTMAS AROUND THE WORLD

Publication Listing

Code #	Title and Grade
SSC1-12	A Time of Plenty Gr. 2
SSN1-92	Abel's Island NS 4-6
SSF1-16	Aboriginal Peoples of Canada Gr. 7-8
SSK1-31	Addition & Subtraction Drills Gr. 1-3
SSK1-28	Addition Drills Gr. 1-3
SSY1-04	Addition Gr. 1-3
SSN1-174	Adv. of Huckle Berry Finn NS 7-8
SSB1-63	African Animals Gr 4-6
SSB1-29	All About Bears Gr. 1-2
SSF1-08	All About Boats Gr. 2-3
SSJ1-02	All About Canada Gr. 2
SSB1-54	All About Cattle Gr. 4-6
SSN1-10	All About Colours Gr. P-1
SSB1-93	All About Dinosaurs Gr. 2
SSN1-14	All About Dragons Gr. 3-5
SSB1-07	All About Elephants Gr. 3-4
SSB1-68	All About Fish Gr. 4-6
SSN1-39	All About Giants Gr. 2-3
SSH1-15	All About Jobs Gr. 1-3
SSH1-05	All About Me Gr. 1
SSA1-02	All About Mexico Gr. 4-6
SSR1-28	All About Nouns Gr. 5-7
SSF1-09	All About Planes Gr. 2-3
SSB1-33	All About Plants Gr. 2-3
SSR1-29	All About Pronouns Gr. 5-7
SSB1-12	All About Rabbits Gr. 2-3
SSB1-58	All About Spiders Gr. 4-6
SSA1-03	All About the Desert Gr. 4-6
SSA1-04	All About the Ocean Gr. 5-7
SSZ1-01	All About the Olympics Gr. 2-4
SSB1-49	All About the Sea Gr. 4-6
SSK1-06	All About Time Gr. 4-6
SSF1-07	All About Trains Gr. 2-3
SSH1-18	All About Transportation Gr. 2
SSB1-01	All About Trees Gr. 4-6
SSB1-61	All About Weather Gr. 7-8
SSB1-06	All About Whales Gr. 3-4
SSPC-26	All Kinds of Clocks B/W Pictures
SSB1-110	All Kinds of Structures Gr. 1
SSH1-19	All Kinds of Vehicles Gr. 3
SSF1-01	Amazing Aztecs Gr. 4-6
SSB1-92	Amazing Earthworms Gr. 2-3
SSJ1-50	Amazing Facts in Cdn History Gr. 4-6
SSB1-32	Amazing Insects Gr. 4-6
SSN1-132	Amelia Bedelia–Camping NS 1-3
SSN1-68	Amelia Bedelia NS 1-3
SSN1-155	Amelia Bedelia-Surprise Shower NS 1-3
SSA1-13	America The Beautiful Gr. 4-6
SSN1-57	Amish Adventure NS 7-8
SSF1-02	Ancient China Gr. 4-6
SSF1-18	Ancient Egypt Gr. 4-6
SSF1-21	Ancient Greece Gr. 4-6
SSF1-19	Ancient Rome Gr. 4-6
SSQ1-06	Animal Town – Big Book Pkg 1-3
SSQ1-02	Animals Prepare Winter- Big Book Pkg 1-3
SSN1-150	Animorphs the Invasion NS 4-6
SSN1-53	Anne of Green Gables NS 7-8
SSB1-40	Apple Celebration Gr. 4-6
SSB1-04	Apple Mania Gr. 2-3
SSB1-38	Apples are the Greatest Gr. P-K
SSB1-59	Arctic Animals Gr. 4-6
SSN1-162	Arnold Lobel Author Study Gr. 2-3
SSPC-22	Australia B/W Pictures
SSA1-05	Australia Gr. 5-8
SSM1-03	Autumn in the Woodlot Gr. 2-3
SSM1-08	Autumn Wonders Gr. 1
SSN1-41	Baby Sister for Frances NS 1-3
SSPC-19	Back to School B/W Pictures
SSC1-33	Back to School Gr. 2-3
SSN1-224	Banner in the Sky NS 7-8
SSN1-36	Bargain for Frances NS 1-3
SSB1-82	Bats Gr. 4-6
SSN1-71	BB – Drug Free Zone NS Gr. 1-3
SSN1-88	BB – In the Freaky House NS 1-3
SSN1-78	BB – Media Madness NS 1-3
SSN1-69	BB – Wheelchair Commando NS 1-3
SSN1-119	Be a Perfect Person-3 Days NS 4-6
SSC1-15	Be My Valentine Gr. 1
SSD1-01	Be Safe Not Sorry Gr. P-1

Code #	Title and Grade
SSN1-09	Bear Tales Gr. 2-4
SSB1-28	Bears Gr. 4-6
SSN1-202	Bears in Literature Gr. 1-3
SSN1-40	Beatrix Potter Gr. 2-4
SSN1-129	Beatrix Potter: Activity Biography 2-4
SSB1-47	Beautiful Bugs Gr. 1
SSB1-21	Beavers Gr. 3-5
SSN1-257	Because of Winn-Dixie NS Gr. 4-6
SSN1-33	Bedtime for Frances NS 1-3
SSN1-114	Best Christmas Pageant Ever NS 4-6
SSN1-32	Best Friends for Frances NS 1-3
SSB1-39	Best Friends Pets Gr. P-K
SSN1-185	BFG NS Gr. 4-6
SSN1-35	Birthday for Frances NS Gr. 1-3
SSN1-107	Borrowers NS Gr. 4-6
SSC1-16	Bouquet of Valentines Gr. 2
SSN1-29	Bread & Jam for Frances NS 1-3
SSN1-63	Bridge to Terabithia NS Gr. 4-6
SSY1-24	BTS Numeración Gr. 1-3
SSY1-25	BTS Adición Gr. 1-3
SSY1-26	BTS Sustracción Gr. 1-3
SSY1-27	BTS Fonética Gr. 1-3
SSY1-28	BTS Leer para Entender Gr. 1-3
SSY1-29	BTS Uso de las Mayúsculas y Reglas de Puntuación Gr. 1-3
SSY1-30	BTS Composición de Oraciones Gr. 1-3
SSY1-31	BTS Composici13n de Historias Gr. 1-3
SSN1-256	Bud, Not Buddy NS Gr. 4-6
SSB1-31	Bugs, Bugs & More Bugs Gr. 2-3
SSR1-07	Building Word Families L.V. 1-2
SSR1-05	Building Word Families S.V. 1-2
SSN1-204	Bunnicula NS Gr. 4-6
SSB1-80	Butterflies & Caterpillars Gr. 1-2
SSN1-164	Call It Courage NS Gr. 7-8
SSN1-67	Call of the Wild NS Gr. 7-8
SSJ1-41	Canada & It's Trading Partners 6-8
SSPC-28	Canada B/W Pictures
SSN1-173	Canada Geese Quilt NS Gr. 4-6
SSJ1-01	Canada Gr. 1
SSJ1-33	Canada's Capital Cities Gr. 4-6
SSJ1-43	Canada's Confederation Gr. 7-8
SSF1-04	Canada's First Nations Gr. 7-8
SSJ1-51	Canada's Landmarks Gr. 1-3
SSJ1-48	Canada's Landmarks Gr. 4-6
SSJ1-42	Canada's Traditions & Celeb. Gr. 1-3
SSB1-45	Canadian Animals Gr. 1-2
SSJ1-37	Canadian Arctic Inuit Gr. 2-3
SSJ1-53	Canadian Black History Gr. 4-8
SSJ1-57	Canadian Comprehension Gr. 1-2
SSJ1-58	Canadian Comprehension Gr. 3-4
SSJ1-59	Canadian Comprehension Gr. 5-6
SSJ1-46	Canadian Industries Gr. 4-6
SSK1-12	Canadian Problem Solving Gr. 4-6
SSJ1-38	Canadian Provinces & Terr. Gr. 4-6
SSY1-07	Capitalization & Punctuation Gr. 1-3
SSN1-198	Captain Courageous NS Gr. 7-8
SSK1-11	Cars Problem Solving Gr. 3-4
SSN1-154	Castle in the Attic NS Gr. 4-6
SSF1-31	Castles & Kings Gr. 4-6
SSN1-144	Cat Ate My Gymsuit NS Gr. 4-6
SSPC-38	Cats B/W Pictures
SSB1-50	Cats – Domestic & Wild Gr. 4-6
SSN1-34	Cats in Literature Gr. 3-6
SSN1-212	Cay NS Gr. 7-8
SSM1-09	Celebrate Autumn Gr. 4-6
SSC1-39	Celebrate Christmas Gr. 4-6
SSC1-31	Celebrate Easter Gr. 4-6
SSC1-23	Celebrate Shamrock Day Gr. 2
SSM1-11	Celebrate Spring Gr. 4-6
SSC1-13	Celebrate Thanksgiving R. 3-4
SSM1-06	Celebrate Winter Gr. 4-6
SSB1-107	Cells, Tissues & Organs Gr. 7-8
SSB1-101	Characteristics of Flight Gr. 4-6
SSN1-66	Charlie & Chocolate Factory NS 4-6
SSN1-23	Charlotte's Web NS Gr. 4-6
SSB1-37	Chicks N'Ducks Gr. 2-4
SSA1-09	China Today Gr. 5-8
SSN1-70	Chocolate Fever NS Gr. 4-6
SSN1-241	Chocolate Touch NS Gr. 4-6
SSC1-38	Christmas Around the World Gr. 4-6
SSPC-42	Christmas B/W Pictures
SST1-08A	Christmas Gr. JK/SK
SST1-08B	Christmas Gr. 1
SST1-08C	Christmas Gr. 2-3
SSC1-04	Christmas Magic Gr. 1
SSC1-03	Christmas Tales Gr. 2-3
SSG1-06	Cinematography Gr. 5-8
SSPC-13	Circus B/W Pictures
SSF1-03	Circus Magic Gr. 3-4
SSJ1-52	Citizenship/Immigration Gr. 4-8

Code #	Title and Grade
SSN1-104	Classical Poetry Gr. 7-12
SSN1-227	Color Gr. 1-3
SSN1-203	Colour Gr. 1-3
SSN1-135	Come Back Amelia Bedelia NS 1-3
SSH1-11	Community Helpers Gr. 1-3
SSK1-02	Concept Cards & Activities Gr. P-1
SSN1-183	Copper Sunrise NS Gr. 7-8
SSN1-86	Corduroy & Pocket Corduroy NS 1-3
SSN1-124	Could Dracula Live in Wood NS 4-6
SSN1-148	Cowboy's Don't Cry NS Gr. 7-8
SSR1-01	Creativity with Food Gr. 4-8
SSB1-34	Creatures of the Sea Gr. 2-4
SSN1-208	Curse of the Viking Grave NS 7-8
SSN1-134	Danny Champion of World NS 4-6
SSN1-98	Danny's Run NS Gr. 7-8
SSK1-21	Data Management Gr. 4-6
SSB1-53	Dealing with Dinosaurs Gr. 4-6
SSN1-178	Dear Mr. Henshaw NS Gr. 4-6
SSB1-22	Deer Gr. 3-5
SSPC-20	Desert B/W Pictures
SSJ1-40	Development of Western Canada 7-8
SSA1-16	Development of Manufacturing 7-9
SSN1-105	Dicken's Christmas NS Gr. 7-8
SSN1-62	Different Dragons NS Gr. 4-6
SSPC-21	Dinosaurs B/W Pictures
SSB1-16	Dinosaurs Gr. 1
SST1-02A	Dinosaurs Gr. JK/SK
SST1-02B	Dinosaurs Gr. 1
SST1-02 C	Dinosaurs Gr. 2-3
SSN1-175	Dinosaurs in Literature Gr. 1-3
SSJ1-26	Discover Nova Scotia Gr. 5-7
SSJ1-36	Discover Nunavut Territory Gr. 5-7
SSJ1-25	Discover Ontario Gr. 5-7
SSJ1-24	Discover PEI Gr. 5-7
SSJ1-22	Discover Québec Gr. 5-7
SSL1-01	Discovering the Library Gr. 2-3
SSB1-106	Diversity of Living Things Gr. 4-6
SSK1-27	Division Drills Gr. 4-6
SSB1-30	Dogs – Wild & Tame Gr. 4-6
SSPC-31	Dogs B/W Pictures
SSN1-196	Dog's Don't Tell Jokes NS Gr. 4-6
SSN1-182	Door in the Wall NS Gr. 4-6
SSB1-87	Down by the Sea Gr. 1-3
SSN1-189	Dr. Jeckyll & Mr. Hyde NS Gr. 4-6
SSG1-07	Dragon Trivia Gr. P-8
SSN1-102	Dragon's Egg NS Gr. 4-6
SSN1-16	Dragons in Literature Gr. 3-6
SSC1-06	Early Christmas Gr. 3-5
SSB1-109	Earth's Crust Gr. 6-8
SSC1-21	Easter Adventures Gr. 3-4
SSC1-17	Easter Delights Gr. P-K
SSC1-19	Easter Surprises Gr. 1
SSPC-12	Egypt B/W Pictures
SSN1-255	Egypt Game NS Gr. 4-6
SSF1-28	Egyptians Today & Yesterday Gr. 2-3
SSJ1-49	Elections in Canada Gr. 4-8
SSB1-108	Electricity Gr. 4-6
SSN1-02	Elves & the Shoemaker NS Gr. 1-3
SSH1-14	Emotions Gr. P-2
SSB1-85	Energy Gr. 4-6
SSN1-108	English Language Gr. 10-12
SSN1-156	Enjoying Eric Wilson Series Gr. 5-7
SSB1-64	Environment Gr. 4-6
SSR1-12	ESL Teaching Ideas Gr. K-8
SSN1-258	Esperanza Rising NS Gr. 4-6
SSR1-22	Exercises in Grammar Gr. 6
SSR1-23	Exercises in Grammar Gr. 7
SSR1-24	Exercises in Grammar Gr. 8
SSF1-20	Exploration Gr. 4-6
SSF1-15	Explorers & Mapmakers of Can. 7-8
SSJ1-54	Exploring Canada Gr. 1-3
SSJ1-56	Exploring Canada Gr. 1-6
SSJ1-55	Exploring Canada Gr. 4-6
SSH1-20	Exploring My School & Community 1
SSPC-39	Fables B/W Pictures
SSN1-15	Fables Gr. 4-6
SSN1-04	Fairy Tale Magic Gr. 3-5
SSPC-11	Fairy Tales B/W Pictures
SSN1-11	Fairy Tales Gr. 1-2
SSN1-199	Family Under the Bridge NS 4-6
SSPC-41	Famous Canadians B/W Pictures
SSJ1-12	Famous Canadians Gr. 4-8
SSN1-210	Fantastic Mr. Fox NS Gr. 4-6
SSB1-36	Fantastic Plants Gr. 4-6
SSPC-04	Farm Animals B/W Pictures
SSB1-15	Farm Animals Gr. 1-2
SST1-03A	Farm Gr. JK/SK
SST1-03B	Farm Gr. 1
SST1-03C	Farm Gr. 2-3
SSJ1-05	Farming Community Gr. 3-4
SSB1-44	Farmyard Friends Gr. P-K
SSJ1-45	Fathers of Confederation Gr. 4-8

Code #	Title and Grade
SSB1-19	Feathered Friends Gr. 4-6
SST1-05A	February Gr. JK/SK
SST1-05B	February Gr. 1
SST1-05C	February Gr. 2-3
SSN1-03	Festival of Fairytales Gr. 3-5
SSC1-36	Festivals Around the World Gr. 2-3
SSN1-168	First 100 Sight Words Gr. 1
SSC1-32	First Days at School Gr. 1
SSJ1-06	Fishing Community Gr. 3-4
SSN1-170	Flowers for Algernon NS Gr. 7-8
SSN1-128	Fly Away Home NS Gr. 4-6
SSD1-05	Food: Fact, Fun & Fiction Gr. 1-3
SSD1-06	Food: Nutrition & Invention Gr. 4-6
SSB1-118	Force and Motion Gr. 1-3
SSB1-119	Force and Motion Gr. 4-6
SSB1-25	Foxes Gr. 3-5
SSN1-172	Freckle Juice NS Gr. 1-3
SSB1-43	Friendly Frogs Gr. 1
SSB1-89	Fruits & Seeds Gr. 4-6
SSN1-137	Fudge-a-Mania NS Gr. 4-6
SSB1-14	Fun on the Farm Gr. 3-4
SSR1-49	Fun with Phonics Gr. 1-3
SSPC-06	Garden Flowers B/W Pictures
SSK1-03	Geometric Shapes Gr. 2-5
SSC1-18	Get the Rabbit Habit Gr. 1-2
SSN1-209	Giver, The NS Gr. 7-8
SSN1-190	Go Jump in the Pool NS Gr. 4-6
SSG1-03	Goal Setting Gr. 6-8
SSG1-08	Gr. 3 Test – Parent Guide
SSG1-99	Gr. 3 Test – Teacher Guide
SSG1-09	Gr. 6 Language Test–Parent Guide
SSG1-97	Gr. 6 Language Test–Teacher Guide
SSG1-10	Gr. 6 Math Test – Parent Guide
SSG1-96	Gr. 6 Math Test – Teacher Guide
SSG1-98	Gr. 6 Math/Lang. Test–Teacher Guide
SSK1-14	Graph for all Seasons Gr. 1-3
SSN1-117	Great Brain NS Gr. 4-6
SSN1-90	Great Expectations NS Gr. 7-8
SSN1-169	Great Gilly Hopkins NS Gr. 4-6
SSN1-197	Great Science Fair Disaster NS 4-6
SSN1-138	Greek Mythology Gr. 7-8
SSN1-113	Green Gables Detectives NS 4-6
SSC1-26	Groundhog Celebration Gr. 2
SSC1-25	Groundhog Day Gr. 1
SSB1-113	Growth & Change in Animals Gr. 2-3
SSB1-114	Growth & Change in Plants Gr. 2-3
SSB1-48	Guinea Pigs & Friends Gr. 3-5
SSB1-104	Habitats Gr. 4-6
SSPC-18	Halloween B/W Pictures
SST1-04A	Halloween Gr. JK/SK
SST1-04B	Halloween Gr. 1
SST1-04C	Halloween Gr. 2-3
SSC1-10	Halloween Gr. 4-6
SSC1-08	Halloween Happiness Gr. 1
SSC1-29	Halloween Spirits Gr. P-K
SSC1-42	Happy Valentines Day Gr. 3
SSN1-205	Harper Moon NS Gr. 7-8
SSN1-123	Harriet the Spy NS Gr. 4-6
SSC1-11	Harvest Time Wonders Gr. 1
SSN1-136	Hatchet NS Gr. 7-8
SSC1-09	Haunting Halloween Gr. 2-3
SSN1-91	Hawk & Stretch NS Gr. 4-6
SSC1-30	Hearts & Flowers Gr. P-K
SSN1-22	Heidi NS Gr. 4-6
SSN1-120	Help I'm Trapped in My NS 4-6
SSN1-24	Henry & the Clubhouse NS 4-6
SSN1-184	Hobbit NS Gr. 7-8
SSN1-122	Hoboken Chicken Emerg. NS 4-6
SSN1-250	Holes NS Gr. 4-6
SSN1-116	How Can a Frozen Detective NS 4-6
SSN1-89	How Can I be a Detective if I NS 4-6
SSN1-96	How Come the Best Clues... NS 4-6
SSN1-133	How To Eat Fried Worms NS 4-6
SSR1-48	How To Give a Presentation Gr. 4-6
SSN1-125	How To Teach Writing Through 7-9
SSR1-10	How To Write a Composition 6-10
SSR1-09	How To Write a Paragraph 5-10
SSR1-08	How To Write an Essay Gr. 7-12
SSR1-03	How To Write Poetry & Stories 4-6
SSD1-07	Human Body Gr. 2-4
SSD1-02	Human Body Gr. 4-6
SSN1-25	I Want to Go Home NS Gr. 4-6
SSH1-06	I'm Important Gr. 2-3
SSH1-07	I'm Unique Gr. 4-6
SSF1-05	In Days of Yore Gr. 4-6
SSF1-06	In Pioneer Days Gr. 2-4
SSM1-10	In the Wintertime Gr. 2
SSB1-41	Incredible Dinosaurs Gr. P-1
SSN1-177	Incredible Journey NS Gr. 4-6
SSN1-100	Indian in the Cupboard NS Gr. 4-6
SSPC-05	Insects B/W Pictures
SSPC-10	Inuit B/W Pictures

Publication Listing

Code #	Title and Grade
SSJ1-10	Inuit Community Gr. 3-4
SSN1-85	Ira Sleeps Over NS Gr. 1-3
SSN1-93	Iron Man NS Gr. 4-6
SSN1-193	Island of the Blue Dolphins NS 4-6
SSB1-11	It's a Dogs World Gr. 2-3
SSM1-05	It's a Marshmallow World Gr. 3
SSK1-05	It's About Time Gr. 2-4
SSC1-41	It's Christmas Time Gr. 3
SSH1-04	It's Circus Time Gr. 1
SSC1-43	It's Groundhog Day Gr. 3
SSB1-75	It's Maple Syrup Time Gr. 2-4
SSC1-40	It's Trick or Treat Time Gr. 2
SSN1-65	James & The Giant Peach NS 4-6
SSN1-106	Jane Eyre NS Gr. 7-8
SSPC-25	Japan B/W Pictures
SSA1-06	Japan Gr. 5-8
SSC1-05	Joy of Christmas Gr. 2
SSN1-161	Julie of the Wolves NS Gr. 7-8
SSB1-81	Jungles Gr. 2-3
SSE1-02	Junior Music for Fall Gr. 4-6
SSE1-05	Junior Music for Spring Gr. 4-6
SSE1-06	Junior Music for Winter Gr. 4-6
SSN1-151	Kate NS Gr. 4-6
SSN1-95	Kidnapped in the Yukon NS Gr. 4-6
SSN1-140	Kids at Bailey School Gr. 2-4
SSN1-176	King of the Wind NS Gr. 4-6
SSF1-29	Klondike Gold Rush Gr. 4-6
SSF1-33	Labour Movement in Canada Gr. 7-8
SSN1-152	Lamplighter NS Gr. 4-6
SSB1-98	Learning About Dinosaurs Gr. 3
SSN1-38	Learning About Giants Gr. 4-6
SSK1-22	Learning About Measurement Gr. 1-3
SSB1-46	Learning About Mice Gr. 3-5
SSK1-09	Learning About Money CDN Gr. 1-3
SSK1-19	Learning About Money USA Gr. 1-3
SSK1-23	Learning About Numbers Gr. 1-3
SSB1-69	Learning About Rocks & Soils Gr. 2-3
SSK1-08	Learning About Shapes Gr. 1-3
SSB1-100	Learning About Simple Machines 1-3
SSK1-04	Learning About the Calendar Gr. 2-3
SSK1-10	Learning About Time Gr. 1-3
SSH1-17	Learning About Transportation Gr. 1
SSB1-02	Leaves Gr. 2-3
SSN1-50	Legends Gr. 4-6
SSC1-27	Lest We Forget Gr. 4-6
SSJ1-13	Let's Look at Canada Gr. 4-6
SSJ1-16	Let's Visit Alberta Gr. 2-4
SSJ1-15	Let's Visit British Columbia Gr. 2-4
SSJ1-03	Let's Visit Canada Gr. 3
SSJ1-18	Let's Visit Manitoba Gr. 2-4
SSJ1-21	Let's Visit New Brunswick Gr. 2-4
SSJ1-27	Let's Visit NFLD & Labrador Gr. 2-4
SSJ1-30	Let's Visit North West Terr. Gr. 2-4
SSJ1-20	Let's Visit Nova Scotia Gr. 2-4
SSJ1-34	Let's Visit Nunavut Gr. 2-4
SSJ1-17	Let's Visit Ontario Gr. 2-4
SSQ1-08	Let's Visit Ottawa Big Book Pkg 1-3
SSJ1-19	Let's Visit PEI Gr. 2-4
SSJ1-31	Let's Visit Québec Gr. 2-4
SSJ1-14	Let's Visit Saskatchewan Gr. 2-4
SSJ1-28	Let's Visit Yukon Gr. 2-4
SSN1-130	Life & Adv. of Santa Claus NS 7-8
SSB1-10	Life in a Pond Gr. 3-4
SSF1-30	Life in the Middle Ages Gr. 7-8
SSB1-103	Light & Sound Gr. 4-6
SSN1-219	Light in the Forest NS Gr. 7-8
SSN1-121	Light on Hogback Hill NS Gr. 4-6
SSN1-46	Lion, Witch & the Wardrobe NS 4-6
SSR1-51	Literature Response Forms Gr. 1-3
SSR1-52	Literature Response Forms Gr. 4-6
SSN1-28	Little House Big Woods NS 4-6
SSN1-233	Little House on the Prairie NS 4-6
SSN1-111	Little Women NS Gr. 7-8
SSN1-115	Live from the Fifth Grade NS 4-6
SSN1-141	Look Through My Window NS 4-6
SSN1-112	Look! Visual Discrimination Gr. P-1
SSN1-61	Lost & Found NS Gr. 4-6
SSN1-109	Lost in the Barrens NS Gr. 7-8
SSJ1-08	Lumbering Community Gr. 3-4
SSN1-167	Magic School Bus Gr. 1-3
SSN1-247	Magic Treehouse Gr. 1-3
SSB1-78	Magnets Gr. 3-5
SSD1-03	Making Sense of Our Senses K-1
SSN1-146	Mama's Going to Buy You a NS 4-6
SSB1-94	Mammals Gr. 1
SSB1-95	Mammals Gr. 2
SSB1-96	Mammals Gr. 3
SSB1-97	Mammals Gr. 5-6
SSN1-160	Maniac Magee NS Gr. 4-6
SSA1-19	Mapping Activities & Outlines! 4-8
SSA1-17	Mapping Skills Gr. 1-3

Code #	Title and Grade
SSA1-07	Mapping Skills Gr. 4-6
SST1-10A	March Gr. JK/SK
SST1-10B	March Gr. 1
SST1-10C	March Gr. 2-3
SSB1-57	Marvellous Marsupials Gr. 4-6
SSK1-01	Math Signs & Symbols Gr. 1-3
SSB1-116	Matter & Materials Gr. 1-3
SSB1-117	Matter & Materials Gr. 4-6
SSH1-03	Me, I'm Special! Gr. P-1
SSK1-16	Measurement Gr. 4-8
SSC1-02	Medieval Christmas Gr. 4-6
SSPC-09	Medieval Life B/W Pictures
SSC1-07	Merry Christmas Gr. P-K
SSK1-15	Metric Measurement Gr. 4-8
SSN1-13	Mice in Literature Gr. 3-5
SSB1-70	Microscopy Gr. 4-6
SSN1-180	Midnight Fox NS Gr. 4-6
SSN1-243	Midwife's Apprentice NS Gr. 4-6
SSJ1-07	Mining Community Gr. 3-4
SSK1-17	Money Talks – Cdn Gr. 3-6
SSK1-18	Money Talks – USA Gr. 3-6
SSB1-56	Monkeys & Apes Gr. 4-6
SSN1-43	Monkeys in Literature Gr. 2-4
SSN1-54	Monster Mania Gr. 4-6
SSN1-97	Mouse & the Motorcycle NS 4-6
SSN1-94	Mr. Poppers Penguins NS Gr. 4-6
SSN1-201	Mrs. Frisby & Rats NS Gr. 4-6
SSR1-13	Milti-Level Spelling Program Gr. 3-6
SSR1-26	Multi-Level Spelling USA Gr. 3-6
SSK1-31	Addition & Subtraction Drills 1-3
SSK1-32	Multiplication & Division Drills 4-6
SSK1-30	Multiplication Drills Gr. 4-6
SSA1-14	My Country! The USA! Gr. 2-4
SSN1-186	My Side of the Mountain NS 7-8
SSN1-58	Mysteries, Monsters & Magic Gr. 6-8
SSN1-37	Mystery at Blackrock Island NS 7-8
SSN1-80	Mystery House NS 4-6
SSN1-157	Nate the Great & Sticky Case NS 1-3
SSF1-23	Native People of North America 4-6
SSF1-25	New France Part 1 Gr. 7-8
SSF1-27	New France Part 2 Gr. 7-8
SSA1-10	New Zealand Gr. 4-8
SSN1-51	Newspapers Gr. 5-8
SSN1-47	No Word for Goodbye NS Gr. 7-8
SSPC-03	North American Animals B/W Pictures
SSF1-22	North American Natives Gr. 2-4
SSN1-75	Novel Ideas Gr. 4-6
SST1-06A	November JK/SK
SST1-06B	November Gr. 1
SST1-06C	November Gr. 2-3
SSN1-244	Number the Stars NS Gr. 4-6
SSY1-03	Numeration Gr. 1-3
SSPC-14	Nursery Rhymes B/W Pictures
SSN1-12	Nursery Rhymes Gr. P-1
SSN1-59	On the Banks of Plum Creek NS 4-6
SSN1-220	One in Middle Green Kangaroo NS 1-3
SSN1-145	One to Grow On NS Gr. 4-6
SSB1-27	Opossums Gr. 3-5
SSJ1-23	Ottawa Gr. 7-9
SSJ1-39	Our Canadian Governments Gr. 5-8
SSF1-14	Our Global Heritage Gr. 4-6
SSH1-12	Our Neighbourhoods Gr. 4-6
SSB1-72	Our Trash Gr. 2-3
SSB1-51	Our Universe Gr. 5-8
SSB1-86	Outer Space Gr. 1-2
SSA1-18	Outline Maps of the World Gr. 1-8
SSB1-67	Owls Gr. 4-6
SSN1-31	Owls in the Family NS Gr. 4-6
SSL1-02	Oxbridge Owl & The Library Gr. 4-6
SSB1-71	Pandas, Polar & Penguins Gr. 4-6
SSN1-52	Paperbag Princess NS Gr. 1-3
SSR1-11	Passion of Jesus: A Play Gr. 7-8
SSA1-12	Passport to Adventure Gr. 4-5
SSR1-06	Passport to Adventure Gr. 7-8
SSR1-04	Personal Spelling Dictionary Gr. 2-5
SSPC-29	Pets B/W Pictures
SSE1-03	Phantom of the Opera Gr. 7-9
SSN1-171	Phoebe Gilman Author Study Gr. 2-3
SSY1-06	Phonics Gr. 1-3
SSN1-237	Pierre Berton Author Study Gr. 7-8
SSN1-179	Pigman NS Gr. 7-8
SSN1-48	Pigs in Literature Gr. 2-4
SSN1-99	Pinballs NS Gr. 4-6
SSN1-60	Pippi Longstocking NS Gr. 4-6
SSF1-12	Pirates Gr. 4-6
SSK1-13	Place Value Gr. 4-6
SSB1-77	Planets Gr. 3-6
SSR1-74	Poetry Prompts Gr. 1-3
SSR1-75	Poetry Prompts Gr. 4-6
SSB1-66	Popcorn Fun Gr. 2-3
SSB1-20	Porcupines Gr. 3-5
SSF1-24	Prehistoric Times Gr. 4-6

Code #	Title and Grade
SSE1-01	Primary Music for Fall Gr. 1-3
SSE1-04	Primary Music for Spring Gr. 1-3
SSE1-07	Primary Music for Winter Gr. 1-3
SSJ1-47	Prime Ministers of Canada Gr. 4-8
SSK1-20	Probability & Inheritance Gr. 7-10
SSN1-49	Question of Loyalty NS Gr. 7-8
SSN1-26	Rabbits in Literature Gr. 2-4
SSB1-17	Raccoons Gr. 3-5
SSN1-207	Radio Fifth Grade NS Gr. 4-6
SSB1-52	Rainbow of Colours Gr. 4-6
SSN1-144	Ramona Quimby Age 8 NS 4-6
SSJ1-09	Ranching Community Gr. 3-4
SSY1-08	Reading for Meaning Gr. 1-3
SSN1-165	Reading Response Forms Gr. 1-3
SSN1-239	Reading Response Forms Gr. 4-6
SSN1-234	Reading with Arthur Gr. 1-3
SSN1-249	Reading with Canadian Authors 1-3
SSN1-200	Reading with Curious George Gr. 2-4
SSN1-230	Reading with Eric Carle Gr. 1-3
SSN1-251	Reading with Kenneth Oppel Gr. 4-6
SSN1-127	Reading with Mercer Mayer Gr. 1-2
SSN1-07	Reading with Motley Crew Gr. 2-3
SSN1-142	Reading with Robert Munsch 1-3
SSN1-06	Reading with the Super Sleuths 4-6
SSN1-08	Reading with the Ziggles Gr. 1
SST1-11A	Red Gr. JK/SK
SSN1-147	Refuge NS Gr. 7-8
SSC1-44	Remembrance Day Gr. 1-3
SSPC-23	Reptiles B/W Pictures
SSB1-42	Reptiles Gr. 4-6
SSN1-110	Return of the Indian NS Gr. 4-6
SSN1-225	River NS Gr. 7-8
SSE1-08	Robert Schuman, Composer Gr. 6-9
SSN1-83	Robot Alert NS Gr. 4-6
SSB1-65	Rocks & Minerals Gr. 4-6
SSN1-149	Romeo & Juliet NS Gr. 7-8
SSB1-88	Romping Reindeer Gr. K-3
SSN1-21	Rumplestiltskin NS Gr. 1-3
SSN1-153	Runaway Ralph NS Gr. 4-6
SSN1-103	Sadako & 1000 Paper Cranes NS 4-6
SSD1-04	Safety Gr. 2-4
SSN1-42	Sarah Plain & Tall NS Gr. 4-6
SSC1-34	School in September Gr. 4-6
SSPC-01	Sea Creatures B/W Pictures
SSB1-79	Sea Creatures Gr. 1-3
SSN1-64	Secret Garden NS Gr. 4-6
SSB1-90	Seeds & Weeds Gr. 2-3
SSY1-02	Sentence Writing Gr. 1-3
SST1-07A	September JK/SK
SST1-07B	September Gr. 1
SST1-07C	September Gr. 2-3
SSN1-30	Serendipity Series Gr. 3-5
SSC1-22	Shamrocks on Parade Gr. 1
SSC1-24	Shamrocks, Harps & Shillelaghs 3-4
SSR1-66	Shakespeare Shorts-Perf Arts Gr. 1-4
SSR1-67	Shakespeare Shorts-Perf Arts Gr. 4-6
SSR1-68	Shakespeare Shorts-Lang Arts Gr. 2-4
SSR1-69	Shakespeare Shorts-Lang Arts Gr. 4-6
SSB1-74	Sharks Gr. 4-6
SSN1-158	Shiloh NS Gr. 4-6
SSN1-84	Sideways Stories Wayside NS 4-6
SSN1-181	Sight Words Activities Gr. 1
SSB1-99	Simple Machines Gr. 4-6
SSN1-19	Sixth Grade Secrets 4-6
SSG1-04	Skill Building with Slates Gr. K-8
SSN1-118	Skinny Bones NS Gr. 4-6
SSB1-24	Skunks Gr. 3-5
SSN1-191	Sky is Falling NS Gr. 4-6
SSB1-83	Slugs & Snails Gr. 1-3
SSB1-55	Snakes Gr. 4-6
SST1-12A	Snow Gr. JK/SK
SST1-12B	Snow Gr. 1
SST1-12C	Snow Gr. 2-3
SSB1-76	Solar System Gr. 4-6
SSPC-44	South America B/W Pictures
SSA1-11	South America Gr. 4-6
SSB1-05	Space Gr. 2-3
SSR1-34	Spelling Blacklines Gr. 1
SSR1-35	Spelling Blacklines Gr. 2
SSR1-14	Spelling Gr. 1
SSR1-15	Spelling Gr. 2
SSR1-16	Spelling Gr. 3
SSR1-17	Spelling Gr. 4
SSR1-18	Spelling Gr. 5
SSR1-19	Spelling Gr. 6
SSR1-27	Spelling Worksavers #1 Gr. 3-5
SSM1-02	Spring Celebration Gr. 2-3
SST1-01A	Spring Gr. JK/SK
SST1-01B	Spring Gr. 1
SST1-01C	Spring Gr. 2-3
SSM1-01	Spring in the Garden Gr. 1-2
SSB1-26	Squirrels Gr. 3-5

Code #	Title and Grade
SSB1-112	Stable Structures & Mechanisms 3
SSG1-05	Steps in the Research Process 5-8
SSG1-02	Stock Market Gr. 7-8
SSN1-139	Stone Fox NS Gr. 4-6
SSN1-214	Stone Orchard NS Gr. 7-8
SSN1-01	Story Book Land of Witches Gr. 2-3
SSR1-64	Story Starters Gr. 1-3
SSR1-65	Story Starters Gr. 4-6
SSR1-73	Story Starters Gr. 1-6
SSY1-09	Story Writing Gr. 1-3
SSB1-111	Structures, Mechanisms & Motion 2
SSN1-211	Stuart Little NS Gr. 4-6
SSK1-29	Subtraction Drills Gr. 1-3
SSY1-05	Subtraction Gr. 1-3
SSY1-11	Successful Language Pract. Gr. 1-3
SSY1-12	Successful Math Practice Gr. 1-3
SSW1-09	Summer Learning Gr. K-1
SSW1-10	Summer Learning Gr. 1-2
SSW1-11	Summer Learning Gr. 2-3
SSW1-12	Summer Learning Gr. 3-4
SSW1-13	Summer Learning Gr. 4-5
SSW1-14	Summer Learning Gr. 5-6
SSN1-159	Summer of the Swans NS Gr. 4-6
SSZ1-02	Summer Olympics Gr. 4-6
SSM1-07	Super Summer Gr. 1-2
SSN1-18	Superfudge NS Gr. 4-6
SSA1-08	Switzerland Gr. 4-6
SSN1-20	T.V. Kid NS. Gr. 4-6
SSA1-15	Take a Trip to Australia Gr. 2-3
SSB1-102	Taking Off With Flight Gr. 1-3
SSN1-55	Tales of the Fourth Grade NS 4-6
SSN1-188	Taste of Blackberries NS Gr. 4-6
SSK1-07	Teaching Math Through Sports 6-9
SST1-09A	Thanksgiving JK/SK
SST1-09C	Thanksgiving Gr. 2-3
SSN1-77	There's a Boy in the Girls... NS 4-6
SSN1-143	This Can't Be Happening NS 4-6
SSN1-05	Three Billy Goats Gruff NS Gr. 1-3
SSN1-72	Ticket to Curlew NS Gr. 4-6
SSN1-82	Timothy of the Cay NS Gr. 7-8
SSF1-32	Titanic Gr. 4-6
SSN1-222	To Kill a Mockingbird NS Gr. 7-8
SSN1-195	Toilet Paper Tigers NS Gr. 4-6
SSJ1-35	Toronto Gr. 4-8
SSH1-02	Toy Shelf Gr. P-K
SSPC-24	Toys B/W Pictures
SSN1-163	Traditional Poetry Gr. 7-10
SSH1-13	Transportation Gr. 4-6
SSW1-01	Transportation Snip Art
SSB1-03	Trees Gr. 2-3
SSA1-01	Tropical Rainforest Gr. 4-6
SSN1-56	Trumpet of the Swan NS Gr. 4-6
SSN1-81	Tuck Everlasting NS Gr. 4-6
SSN1-126	Turtles in Literature Gr. 1-3
SSN1-45	Underground to Canada NS 4-6
SSN1-27	Unicorns in Literature Gr. 3-5
SSJ1-44	Upper & Lower Canada Gr. 7-8
SSN1-192	Using Novels Canadian North Gr. 7-8
SSC1-14	Valentines Day Gr. 5-8
SSPC-45	Vegetables B/W Pictures
SSY1-01	Very Hungry Caterpillar NS 30/Pkg 1-3
SSF1-13	Victorian Era Gr. 7-8
SSC1-35	Victorian Christmas Gr. 5-8
SSF1-17	Viking Age Gr. 4-6
SSN1-206	War with Grandpa SN Gr. 4-6
SSB1-91	Water Gr. 2-4
SSN1-166	Watership Down NS Gr. 7-8
SSH1-16	Ways We Travel Gr. P-K
SSN1-101	Wayside Sch. Little Stranger NS 4-6
SSN1-76	Wayside Sch. is Falling Down NS 4-6
SSB1-60	Weather Gr. 4-6
SSN1-17	Wee Folk in Literature Gr. 3-5
SSPC-08	Weeds B/W Pictures
SSQ1-04	Welcome Back – Big Book Pkg 1-3
SSB1-73	Whale Preservation Gr. 5-8
SSH1-08	What is a Community? Gr. 2-4
SSH1-01	What is a Family? Gr. 2-3
SSH1-09	What is a School? Gr. 1-2
SSJ1-32	What is Canada? Gr. P-K
SSN1-79	What is RAD? Read & Discover 2-4
SSB1-62	What is the Weather Today? Gr. 2-4
SSN1-194	What's a Daring Detective NS 4-6
SSH1-10	What's My Number Gr. P-K
SSR1-02	What's the Scoop on Words Gr. 4-6
SSN1-73	Where the Red Fern Grows NS 7-8
SSN1-87	Where the Wild Things Are NS 1-3
SSN1-187	Whipping Boy NS Gr. 4-6
SSN1-226	Who is Frances Rain? NS Gr. 4-6
SSN1-74	Who's Got Gertie & How...? NS 4-6
SSN1-131	Why did the Underwear ... NS 4-6
SSC1-28	Why Wear a Poppy? Gr. 2-3
SSJ1-11	Wild Animals of Canada Gr. 2-3

Publication Listing

Code #	Title and Grade	Code #	Title and Grade	Code #	Title and Grade	Code #	Title and Grade
SSPC-07	Wild Flowers B/W Pictures						
SSB1-18	Winter Birds Gr. 2-3						
SSZ1-03	Winter Olympics Gr. 4-6						
SSM1-04	Winter Wonderland Gr. 1						
SSC1-01	Witches Gr. 3-4						
SSN1-213	Wolf Island NS Gr. 1-3						
SSE1-09	Wolfgang Amadeus Mozart 6-9						
SSB1-23	Wolves Gr. 3-5						
SSC1-20	Wonders of Easter Gr. 2						
SSB1-35	World of Horses Gr. 4-6						
SSB1-13	World of Pets Gr. 2-3						
SSF1-26	World War II Gr. 7-8						
SSN1-221	Wrinkle in Time NS Gr. 7-8						
SSPC-02	Zoo Animals B/W Pictures						
SSB1-08	Zoo Animals Gr. 1-2						
SSB1-09	Zoo Celebration Gr. 3-4						